PENSION CLARITY

THE LEADER'S GUIDE TO SMARTER PLANNING FOR OUR FUTURE

M. CATHERINE MILLER

Pension Clarity

PAGE TWO BOOKS

Cataloguing in publication information is available from Library and Archives Canada.

ISBN 978-1-77458-063-9 (paperback)
ISBN 978-1-77458-064-6 (ebook)

Page Two
pagetwo.com

Edited by Crissy Calhoun
Copyedited by Kendra Ward
Cover design by Jennifer Lum
Interior design by Setareh Ashrafologhalai
and Taysia Louie

marrismiller.com

For my family

CONTENTS

INTRODUCTION

GLOBALIZATION has led to a shift in social, political, and economic factors, which include geo-political and financial boundaries, trans-governmental and local policies, and the nature of resource allocation and regulation, as well as aspects of business and social cultures. Under globalization, the way in which authority and risk control is applied in practice could be said to be changing, and this includes the pension sector.

At the same time, in the pension market, these shifts are not fundamental enough to help companies transform their pension promises quickly. Instead, in the last few years, we've seen many globally significant companies try to rapidly change the way that they manage their pensions in response to downturns in their industries, and we've seen firms accumulate significantly underfunded pensions. But these approaches have more often than not put these companies, and their shareholders, at risk. Bloomberg Markets reported that by the end of 2017, the largest S&P 500 companies' pension funds were facing a $382 billion funding gap. As a case in point, General Electric (GE), although it was sitting on a pension surplus of $14.6 billion in 2001, was running a deficit of $7 billion a mere seven years later, in 2008. By the end of 2016, the GE deficit was $31 billion. One year later, by the end of 2017, the deficit was about $100 billion.[1]

Something has to change. In the new global economy, businesses and organizations need renewed optimism for their pensions. And change is coming: we are seeing expansions in the pension industry and progressive, sustainable solutions that can lead to a different way of thinking about pensions and offer hope for those who want a better way of doing business, or at least a more realistic one.

To build a prosperous future for people, business, and society, leadership has to be at the centre of our decision-making process when creating and sustaining pension plans.

Pension obligations consist of payments owed to current and future retirees, this year and the year after, and the year after that, and far into the future—obligations that should have been advance-funded by paying into the relevant pension funds the amounts needed to cover those benefits, year by year, as those benefits were accrued. Every year that an organization fails to do this, or the pension industry fails to advise on such actions, is a year in which they place obligations on future generations of employees and of the company itself. This is a risk that no leader should be willing to take.

How do we define true leadership in this context of pension transformation? As fairness? Ownership? A will to manage?

We must be realistic about our expectations for pensions.

Leadership means that we need to imagine a different future for the pension market: one in which there is an agreement about what will mitigate risk and keep our people, our organizations, and our global society safe and secure. To this end, trusting that the market will correct itself is no longer enough, as clearly we have proved ourselves incapable of relying on market forces alone. If we are to be a sustainable global society, then we need to create, implement, and monitor regulations that will work in this environment. The current shifts are reflective of our first steps towards this goal, but more needs to be done to ensure a high level of risk management in our pension planning over the long term.

In this book, we'll explore just how to address these insufficiencies and opportunities in pension planning for the future. We'll discover just how much our risk management has to do with leadership, rather than with crunching numbers.

We will cover three essential pension leadership strategies in this book.

1. **How to design your pensions for financial security.** An employer's financial obligation to pension promises is a long journey; the pension promises offered today need to be sustainable throughout the lives of individual members. At the same time, the regulatory landscape is shifting. This offers companies more flexibility, not necessarily more complexity or cost. For example, many companies' existing benefit plan provisions were likely established decades ago: these need to be examined on a regular basis, especially when regulations change. Many expensive options that are adding cost to the plan, but little value, are likely still in your provisions. Employers need to look anew at their defined benefit promises, and focus on funding the most profitable benefits and offloading outdated provisions.

2. **How to create pension plans designed for people, not the experts.** Pensions are misunderstood, both by companies and by employees, partially because their benefits are not clearly communicated. Client letters and employee pension statements are math heavy and full of industry jargon, and most look more like a legal document than like something that people can use. With a simple and pleasant approach to communication, people will understand and appreciate their pension programs. They'll engage in pension processes, and that means they'll act like true stakeholders in the company. Evidence shows

that plans designed for people increase overall accountability for pension performance and have a positive impact on employee performance.

3. **How to build responsiveness into your business environment.** Supporting pension discussions with data brought to the table by experts is important; but even more so, executives need to be able to understand pension benefits and their implications in the moment. Instead of raising questions and then waiting two weeks for a team of pension analysts to come back with answers, leaders can access up-to-date information, trends, and projections easily mined from new HR system technologies. Knowing how to view and use this data can help executives cut through the clutter and focus on strategies that deliver immediate results.

We can make pensions work. But the pervasive, ongoing uncertainty means that organizations need to get their actuaries and pension advisors working in a fundamentally different way. Modern pension design should work for individuals and society while building successful companies at the same time. Pensions are about people, not simply numbers. To build a long-term, sustainable pension plan that's beyond the norm of traditional pension management, we need to think creatively, reflexively, and confidently, and we need to start with leadership.

1

WHAT'S PAST IS PAST

PENSION SUCCESS IS about resilient performance and parity in an age of uncertainty. But pension security, our way of working, and the capital market have become more intertwined than we're willing to admit.

Why is this challenge important? In economic terms, financial security and stability create the peace of mind we feel when we aren't worried about covering our expenses thanks to our reliable income amount. It also means that we have enough money saved to cover emergencies and future goals. Financial security means having enough money for the rest of our lives once we retire from work. Our pensions are meant to deliver that money.

In the past, however, loopholes in corporate and organizational policy frameworks for the pension market have made it difficult, if not impossible, to ensure adequate funds for employee retirement. That's because a pension manager's ability to use business acumen and good judgement affects whether a pension plan will provide after-work financial security for employees.

But before we get to how to provide that security, we need to look to the past to examine what legacies we're dealing with when it comes to pension planning.

The human organization, namely, the ability of a company to recognize the value of its human assets through compensation practices, has been cited by writers in all fields of international business as a key differentiator between those companies that will be successful and those that will not in the next century. A firm's way of managing its employees, including its pension benefits, can give it an advantage over its competitors and lead to positive organizational growth. But, as the examples below show, the reality is that growth has been and is still being leveraged in a way that does not sustain employee needs. No matter what pension plan is developed, attention to accounting practices in pension management will only increase in the wake of widespread challenges associated with the current global economic crisis and the ensuing media criticism of pensions, executive pay packages, and perquisites.

Let's examine some of the challenges that organizations have faced in the last few years and explore why they have been so deeply problematic.

Sears Canada. The Sears Canada pension made headline news in late 2018 because of an underfunded pension plan that seemed to be, according to a lawsuit against

Sears Canada's largest shareholders, created to benefit investors rather than those who contributed to it in the first place. While $509 million in dividends was paid to Sears Canada shareholders in 2013, the pension fund was short $133 million by the time the company shuttered its doors in 2018, according to court documents.[1] In a deal structured in October 2019, pensioners stand to collect about $48 million, which, according to the lawsuit, is less than a tenth of what they should have received as a result of their investment in the company. Nonetheless, Sears did not do anything exceptional; in comparison to its industry, its actions were status quo and the company did not break funding rules. The more damaging challenge to employees, therefore, may be the pensioners' argument that the 2013 dividend payment crippled the retailer's ability to remain in business, because it made it difficult for the company to gain access to liquid capital when it was required.

General Motors. In his book *While America Aged*, Roger Lowenstein describes GM's unsustainable pension promises—which shifted from a symbol of generosity and endearment of the employer to a horrendous debt that all but bankrupted the company—as a warning call.[2] GM built back its pension after a debilitating few years of poor management, with the company closing its Canadian plants, while employees were left confused about what they may have sacrificed in the short term. Active plan members and retirees are likely to be simultaneously relieved that the company recovered and reinvested $1.6 billion in its Canadian pension plans and deeply concerned about GM shutting down its operations. And yet, the company had the pension industry's best and brightest advisors, including actuaries, investment experts, lawyers, and accountants who created a plan that was regulatorily sound. As with Sears Canada, there may be worry that the company has only shifted money from one part of the business to another, leaving employees' needs at the bottom of its concerns. Counting on the market to prosper and fix the issues is a classic mistake.

GE. GE has the largest pension deficit among S&P 500 companies, affecting 600,000 people, and that deficit is $11 billion worse than the next closest company, according to S&P Dow Jones Indices, and likely running close to $50 billion in 2020. It's also going into freefall. Although a pension shortfall now, it was once a surplus of $14.6 billion, in 2001, when Jack Welch retired as CEO. At his leaving, GE decided to put money into mergers and acquisitions instead of keeping it safe for employees. With the company's current cash challenges, it has relied on stock buybacks to try to stem the tide, but this has not resulted in positive changes. GE cashed out at the bottom of the market and created alternative investment plans, and even though the Dow Jones recovered, alternatives did not provide GE the same level of return. New deficits piled up on the old deficit so much that GE's original position was never recovered. In fact, GE's massively underfunded pension may not only be a risk to its existence, and to the livelihood of its employees and retirees, but may also have larger economic implications because of the scale of its operations, should the company fold.[3]

CPP/QPP. Even the Canada and Quebec Pension Plans are going through a major transition. In 2018, it was announced that starting in 2019, Canadians' Canada Pension Plan contributions would increase from 4.95 per cent to 5.1 per cent on earnings between $3,500 and $57,400. It was the first of five years of graduated increases running until 2023, when the rate will reach 5.95 per cent. "You can think of it as a cost right now, but you're actually going to be contributing toward an enhanced Canada Pension Plan benefit over time, ultimately leading to a higher amount of pensionable earnings," said Jamie Golombek, managing director of tax and estate planning with CIBC. "So you're actually going to get something in return for that extra contribution."[4] This increase in contributions is necessary because CPP, like corporate pensions, has become underfunded. The goal of the government, however, is to recognize our changing demographics and the need for a more sustainable retirement plan for Canadians, and these increased contributions are a means to shift the status quo. The Canadian government has chosen to take this route because of the ongoing insecurity in the corporate pension world as well.

These examples illustrate what can happen when deals are made to shortchange the pension system and chronically underfund individual plans. They go well beyond poor financial planning, illustrating the collapse of what we believed were our retirement certainties. In fact, cases such as these don't reveal a lack of financial analysis, but rather a human tendency to stay on the path of least resistance, or, in some cases, a lack of ethical boundaries between the interests of those in leadership positions and those who serve these firms as employees.

There is a bigger issue, however.

Over the last two decades, the concept of retirement has shifted to become an aspirational lifestyle in which we will travel, experience freedom, and generally get all the benefits that we expect. We have also experienced a sociological shift in how we live after the age of sixty-five; few families support the elderly at home, and independence has become the norm. These changes have placed a huge burden on pensions and retirement investments that, because of larger economic forces as well as market shifts, may or may not come through. And when the investments don't generate sufficient income, the finance industry is always eager to offer fixes such as hedge funds and derivatives that can't solve the long-term problem either.

What has to be recognized, no matter how you crunch the numbers, is that today's corporations, as both stock fund providers and pension providers, are taking on more than just the role they did in the past by providing retirement support for the majority of Canadians. Our society relies on pensions to ensure that our retired and elderly community members are safe and secure as they age. Organizations have a responsibility to shift towards equity and to recognize the value of employees.

The pension leadership path forward

The path ahead will be an awakening—a time for pension plan managers to look at seizing opportunities and not just at surmounting challenges. Potential external shocks to the system continue to lurk, and growth cannot be taken for granted.

Successful organizations will have come to terms with the fact that in the new paradigm taking shape around them, some of the old rules simply don't work. Regardless of size and segment, pension funds now need to be nimble, resilient, and easy to understand and upgrade over time. Pension managers need to prepare for uncertainty, and achieve ever-greater value for cost. They need to take an active stance on social issues, satisfy member demands for radical transparency and sustainability, and, most importantly, have the courage to disrupt their own sources and their traditional beliefs to realize these changes and win new generations of workers so that they can better compete in the new global economy.

Major trends are beginning to define the pension agenda.

Ownership

On the investment side, we foresee shifts in understanding what ownership means to pensions: Is the company or the employee the owner of the fund? One of the most important challenges is evolving pension planning from a mechanical exercise based on number-crunching into a transformational-change mentality based on leadership and common sense. More secure and efficient joint governance platforms in which employees have a stake in what can be achieved with their pensions are needed.

Common sense is all about achieving parity. This requires

- understanding controllable risks;
- deliberation about how age, gender, and other social differences affect what people can expect to earn on their pension during their working years; and

- understanding fundamental management challenges in the type of pensions that are chosen, and the systems behind each.

The management of pensions is often focused on the financial makeup of the pension design, when in fact the economic benefit may be better derived from a broader approach that accounts for the macro economy as well as the performance of the firm. Because demographic changes have intensively affected pensions over the last thirty years in particular, pundits posit that it may also be helpful to measure the impact of political and regulatory changes as well as future growth in the development of a pension management program.

Externalities may affect the development and management of funds. Because more and more corporations are putting the onus on their employees to participate in choosing and managing the mutual funds that now make up the majority of their pensions, this must be considered on an ethical level.[5] Pension management research shows that underlying this global movement of participant choice is an implicit assumption about behaviour: that employee-citizens to whom the responsibility of choice has been handed are well-informed economic agents who act rationally to maximize their self-interest. But, as one can clearly understand based on what happens in real-life pension situations, this ideal is not reflected in reality.[6]

Most individual employees make decisions based on emotions rather than on rational thought, which means that pensions are not necessarily the retirement panacea they are thought to be.[7] Overconfidence in their own financial planning abilities means that many people believe they can live well on relatively small asset pools during retirement. Yet after leaving work, they then find they run out of money, sometimes within a few months of retirement. This also means that because employees in Canada will likely not be able to solely rely on the CPP/QPP system, they will need to understand the value of their company pension to their own long-term security. This should be accounted for when managing a pension plan at a corporation.

If human decision making regarding financial planning is flawed, then less risky investment choices may be more ethical components of a well-developed pension program. It is also clear from the research that if an external mutual fund system is used, then companies must create an ethical way to introduce their employees to financial management. Because employees may not be able to choose well for themselves, and because they have been proven to be overconfident, the company must complete due diligence in ensuring that employees understand the choices in funds. A company that follows these recommendations will likely be able to create a sound and sustainable corporate pension strategy.

Sustainability

There is a need to examine ongoing concerns about sustainable returns and how to alleviate pensions' impact on the environment—for example, through investments in oil and gas.[8] More and more pension members and stakeholders will also push for greater transparency into resources and financial security, which makes shared-risk relationships a priority.

Environmental, social, and governance (ESG) refers to the three central factors in measuring the sustainability and ethical impact of an investment in a business. These criteria help determine the future financial performance of companies (return and risk). This means that companies have to re-situate their responsibility to the needs of stakeholders (anyone who is influenced, either directly or indirectly, by the actions of the firm) rather than those of shareholders. It also requires a company to conceive and use a reciprocal social structure that takes the needs of all stakeholders into equal consideration. The company must also invest in sustainable development and business practices, which subject their pension management processes to a higher level of criticism, and will benefit from redefining profit as not simply financial gain but the total benefit enjoyed by the society in which the company operates.

Capitalism is premised on a system of unlimited growth, but this does not mean that it has to use all our environmental resources to achieve this goal. Although there is no theoretical obstacle to profit for a given corporation, companies can shift the way that they invest in pension plans. Capital can acquire more capital, but it is not the case that this capital necessarily has to be sourced from the same value chains as in the past. One can invest capital in extracting natural resources that are not sustainable, or one can invest it in financialization sectors like hedge funds or mortgages that have been bundled together by a bank and sold as shares and traded: both are equally risky and equally able to provide a profit.

But what about the risks?

Five risks are tied to planning pensions *without* sustainability in mind, according to field research:[9]

- **Climate policy risks.** Constraints on the advancement of non-renewable technology means that businesses face new regulations on research, development, supply chain management, and transport, no matter what industry they are in.

- **Commodity price risk.** Take the oil industry as an example. The collapse of oil prices over the last five years means that expensive reserves forming the next phase of expansion in Alberta's north will remain undeveloped. In addition, although a recent decision by OPEC and its allies to cut production by 1.2 million barrels per day should be enough to bring the oil market into balance, this is not sustainable.

- **Energy innovation risk.** Renewable costs for electricity generation in many parts of the world are now about the same or less than those for building new fossil fuel plants, but demand will be growing.
- **Carbon liability risk.** The link between carbon emissions and damages is evolving, and it is possible that in the future carbon producers will be held liable for damages, in the same way that tobacco companies were sued for health damages resulting from use of their products.
- **Community opposition risks.** Global megaprojects and even local developments are facing greater scrutiny than ever before, and it has become the norm to ask whether a project has "social licence" to proceed in a community.

The goal, therefore, for the average company is to become aware of planning processes that aren't modern and ethical and to become open to changing the status quo. The economic gains made from the business principles developed in the past have slowed as it becomes harder and harder to increase production capacity without harmful effects on the world around us. This can affect both a company itself and how it invests on behalf of its employees.

Expectations

Business managers need ever-simple and effective ways to improve their organizations' and their workers' financial wealth.

Wise companies are prepared to disrupt the pension ecosystem, strip down pension ideas to their basic principles, and focus on sustainability to reduce reactive acts that respond to noise instead of trends.

Let's say you have acquired a billion-dollar business and have expectations about how this new division should perform, and how you'll pay off your initial investment. That's what it should feel like when you think of pension plans, which, just like your acquisition, are going to cost you a significant amount of capital. Will you let your plan run wild or will you make sure you have a well-thought-out strategy to manage it?

What we've learned from the examples of the past is that perhaps even the biggest firms should start to manage their pensions like smaller ones do. Think about how this might work. Leaders of a larger company, one that has more assets at hand, may feel as if they are more likely to be able to mitigate the risk of pension investments because they have significant capital assets, whether or not they actually can. At the same time, these institutions may be more likely to take on pension fund risks, knowing that a small loss in one sector is not going to put another sector at risk unnecessarily. More prudent companies will be more likely to invest in less risky assets for their pensions. This means that they will be less likely to encounter both the highs and the lows of the market, because they need to keep more capital in low-risk investments to protect their employees' interests.

In the next chapter, we'll discover what questions we can ask and what purpose we can create for our pensions so that we can mitigate the kind of risks that we've discussed here and instead move towards pensions that work for organizations and employees alike.

2

AVOIDING RISKS, AND THE THREE MOST IMPORTANT QUESTIONS

ACCOUNTING STANDARDS have been dictating pension management behaviours for a long time—in some cases, in a negative, short-term-thinking way.

Until relatively recently, the disclosure requirements for financial statements and the funding requirements for an actuarially sound plan did not match. This means that, because of past accounting standards, the components of pension expense, balance sheet accounts, and the various assumptions that drive these figures didn't report actuarial gains and losses in their net income on statements. There were significant discrepancies between what people assumed about their pensions and what was happening in real terms. Although some shareholders understood this, others didn't.

Accounting standards, even today, are among the factors to blame for much pension trouble, as they can often hide the real problems. Public companies are more affected by disclosure requirements, but the mechanical requirements do not offer a full view of future obligation to assess the value of a pension.

For example, while balanced scorecard assessments can go far in mitigating risk, a better plan may be to deliberately assess risk with its own instrument specific to the pension market. By and large, best practices in mitigating risk start with understanding why decisions made at the top of the firm affect pension choices, rather than focusing on actuarial analysis and pension trends.

More principle-based practices and guidelines of risk management have good intentions, but they can often amount to a checklist exercise that ends up adding cost, not value, for employers. What do you do with the numbers, and what questions do you ask before writing that cheque?

We need a shift in leadership to transform pension dynamics. We have to get away from the mechanics of pension planning and regulations to recognize that the purpose behind pensions, what they provide for the people in a company, determines success. And first and foremost, we need to understand why our business traditions and standard beliefs about pensions put us in harm's way.

How businesses put themselves at risk

Jim Collins's Five Stages of Decline[1] can help illustrate how and why businesses like GM, GE, and Sears Canada take the wrong pension risks and may not be able to maintain their momentum over the long term. The five stages form a rubric that can evaluate just what has gone wrong within a company so that better choices can be made in the future, or how a large corporation can lose so much of its market power that it puts all its stakeholders at risk. We'll use GE's pension as an example.

In Stage 1, which Collins calls *hubris born of success*, companies become used to the fact that they can generate profit and, therefore, they lose sight of what made them successful in the first place. Companies with pensions that start to do well may feel as if they are entitled to be successful, and in this state their leaders may make decisions based on the assumption that they will not change their direction in the long term. As Collins notes, we need to understand why success takes place, rather than assuming that a certain set of practices will guarantee anything other than a short-term run. This is true for pensions, in that having realistic insight in order to avoid ongoing problems is important. Because former GE CEO Jack Welch, as mentioned above, left the company in 2001 in an enviable cultural and financial position with many safety nets in place for the company's many levels of stakeholders, GE was in a place of hubris as it moved into the twenty-first century.[2]

Collins suggests that, in Stage 2, the *undisciplined pursuit of more*, companies are inclined to grow without understanding why or how this can be achieved sustainably. In the modern company, he notes, sustained competitive growth is not as achievable as it was in the past, and even a disciplined company will need a creative change of direction when faced with challenges. Pouring money into a pension is not enough, not a realistic approach. Instead, a company needs to ask itself why it wants to achieve what it believes will make it more successful. Without a reflective practice associated with growth, many companies, Collins suggests, will grow too fast and lack the ability to build true capacity to manage that growth. This leads to a higher level of vulnerability. Because GE was so large, each division had, before 2001, operated like its own company under an overarching mandate, wherein autonomy was expected; new CEO Jeff Immelt wanted to move towards growth and, therefore, he left individual units to operate on their own, as "headquarters became increasingly involved in promoting and supporting developmental initiatives (e.g., Imagination Breakthroughs and Enterprise Selling), so the corporate HQ became more of a partner with the business divisions rather than an overseer of divisional performance and interrogator of business strategies."[3] Less oversight meant more risk, and GE also shifted its focus from products to services in a very short period of time, with services quickly responsible for half of its revenue by 2015.[4]

Collins calls Stage 3 the *denial of risk and peril.* In this stage, some people within the firm may raise the alarm about pension practices that could have a negative long-term effect, and leaders may ignore this information because they want to believe that the company will be fine without spending money on any substantive changes. Information may be very clearly pointing towards a different set of actions, but these facts may be set aside because they are seen as problematic. This situation can lead to a rapid decrease in morale and performance, especially when pensions are at risk; team members see what needs to be done but those in positions of power prefer to keep their heads in the sand. The consequence of these kinds of decisions is that the firm becomes desperate. Immelt wanted to grow the GE business, but he did not rely on the expertise and insight of individual business units and, rather, trusted only his own team to make large-scale decisions about the units. This meant that core facets of the brand's aimed values of sustainability, for example, were set aside; even though concerns were raised about some of the company's choices at the time, there was a decrease in responsiveness, as well as concern about a lack of alignment within the firm and its values.[5]

Collins states that in Stage 4, *grasping for salvation*, a company will be past the point of making internal fixes to slow down the deleterious effects of its earlier poor decision making. In this stage, a company will have to make bold moves to save a pension from its eventual destruction. The company's leaders will have to risk more in order to avoid the impact of the problems that they did not address earlier, which means that there will likely be a significant amount of fallout in terms of layoffs, divestments, or changes in the way that the company is financed. This stage often involves a rapid change in leadership to address pension issues, or an influx of consultants who can do little at this point to stem the tide. Recent news reports about GE state that there is so much financial, social, and market degradation associated with the company that it may not be able to respond in a way that allows the business to keep building.[6] The company has begun to liquidate its assets; in early 2019 it had to sell one of its largest aviation assets in a sudden move to gain capital.

Finally, Collins advises that before Stage 5, *capitulation to irrelevance or death*, a company may have already gone through several rounds of Stage 4 activities. In the final stage, so much financial, social, and market degradation is associated with the company that the pension fund may be its last hope for keeping afloat, and even if the company uses it, it may still not be enough. The company may also just fade away if it does not have any assets left to sell, depending on how it managed its Stage 4 operations.

GE is not yet in this position, but without substantive changes, not only the company's pension but its whole operation will be at risk.

One can see that GE's pension issues aligned with its overarching strategic and market issues: these were not independent problems. As reported in 2020, GE's total debt has nearly tripled since 2013. It owed almost $77 billion as of 2018,[7] and that amount has continued to increase to $90.9 billion as of 2020.[8]

Collins suggests that a company can address such inadequacies if its leaders are willing to admit when they are going in the wrong direction. As he states, it is not inevitable that a company go out of business because it loses its market share or edge; it can choose to operate for a short period of time rather than insist on ongoing growth, it can grow slowly and effectively, and it can adapt by changing its strategies and market models over time. There is not one single path forward, and companies can also make informed decisions about whether they want to push through stagnation or simply close. This does not have to be a battle or have a negative impact if it is done thoughtfully with all stakeholders in mind. But the reality is that GE can no longer achieve this goal.

Move towards leadership and risk management

A small shift in leadership can transform pension dynamics. Leadership is often needed to prioritize pension management findings for each team member involved in decision making. People in a team will not believe in, support, and implement needed changes unless they can see the value of the changes to the organization and to themselves; this is the psychosocial construct of organizational behaviour. To this end, if an organization wants to change how it operates, it will not only have to show people the metrics that it is addressing and expecting, but also create the motivational impetus for change.

Let's look at all of the levels of risk that a company may face in managing its pension:

- Liquidity risk could happen when the organization cannot meet its obligations because of an inability to support normal business activity or regulatory requirements, or endure changes to credit ratings.
- Capital risk could happen when a company is unable to maintain appropriate capital ratios, which could lead to an inability to support business activity.
- Structural risk related to the management of non-contractual risks could happen, primarily arising from the impact on

the organization's balance sheet of changes in interest rates on income, or of foreign exchange rates on capital ratios.

- Credit risk could happen when and if the organization suffers financial loss resulting from its customers, clients, or market counterparties failing to fulfill their contractual obligations.
- Operational risk results from the direct or indirect impact of human factors, inadequate or failed internal systems, or external events.
- Market risk can occur if the company suffers financial loss because of being unable to hedge its balance sheet at prevailing market levels linked to changes in both the level and volatility of prices, interest rates, or foreign exchange rates.

All these risks can affect pensions. That's a reality. But what is it that truly ties all these aspects of business together? Leadership—and the leadership to recognize that people's livelihoods and survival after retirement are at stake.

We can assess the numbers in all these risk scenarios until the end of time, but it won't change how much risk a group takes on unless leadership is committed to lowering the risk threshold for the organization. Pension managers and human resource managers also need to buy into pension changes that allow them to act when and where they see fit. This requires a different way of thinking, one grounded in integrity and emotional awareness.

In practice, this means that listening to team members and reflecting on the issues at hand are important parts of leadership. Although a manager may be expected to make a change happen as quickly as possible, a leader can create space and time to address concerns from the team and provide opportunities for team members to offer critical feedback before any changes are implemented. Although management expectations are often grounded in numerical assessments, leadership expectations are often grounded in the evaluation of human experience and ideas. Everyone in an organization must be able to embody the values of the organization, remain motivated, and engage forward, creative thinking about how to constantly improve.

The three most important questions

To show leadership and build forward momentum in your pension planning right now, you need to be able to answer the following questions.

1. **Why do you have a pension for your employees?** Andrew Carnegie, the early nineteenth-century industrialist, revolutionized pensions as a means to shift the expectations

for retirement in the United States and, later, around the world. Carnegie believed that if people's future financial health was taken care of, then they could focus on their jobs, rather than worry about what the future had in store for them. In 1901, Carnegie established significant pension funds for his former employees at Homestead and later, in 1905, for American college professors—funds that are worth, at present, more than $12 billion and $279 billion, respectively.[9]

Ask yourself why your organization has a pension, and what legacy you would like to leave from this investment. What's your fundamental rationale all about? Increasing the attractiveness of your organization to employees, present or future? Creating a sense of security among team members and building commitment to the job over the long term? Meeting basic expectations for your industry?

2. **What results do you want to get?** Pension managers always hope to get better financial results and improve the way pension work is done, but it's important to raise your expectations. It is possible to create the foundation for a strategic human resource plan using pensions, which decreases attrition, increases retention and knowledge management in the organization, and improves motivation.

   Ask yourself: How can the strategic goals of the organization be furthered through pension planning? How can you motivate and align your employees towards sustainable growth with the right plan of action in mind?

3. **How do you know you will get the results you want?** Your organization needs clarity on how any changes to your pension plan will improve your organization and its performance, and make your employees happy and productive. Not everything has to be measured, but what matters to your strategy has to be evaluated carefully, not once but regularly.

   How can you put the right metrics in place to measure your results? And how will you know whether your work is having the right effect where it matters—inside your organization?

Pensions should be designed for employees. The only way for corporate pensions to succeed is for a business to succeed. If there is no successful business, there will not be a successful pension. Business and actuaries need to work together in a fundamentally new way to improve how we look at and act on pension decisions. That's why corporate pension strategies are the key to adding value and creating a sustainable future.

When shareholders put their capital in an organization, it stimulates employment and business growth. But today's labour and capital have become more intertwined, which makes labour and capital vulnerable. Trillions of dollars in pension capital that workers contributed to and still depend on are at stake.

Although leaders are confident and comfortable in making business strategies that lead to future business growth, they need to clearly understand what works for employees and what can be sustained over the long term. A forward-moving plan considers the people who work for the company above all other stakeholders. Such a plan has to support the diversity of opinions present in a large-scale operation, and respect the ideas of those on the ground working with customers and clients.

The problem is that current solutions are math heavy. We advocate for leaders to take a more commonsensical approach to make a bigger impact on pensions that work for business, individuals, and society, an approach grounded in a realistic assessment of where the business world is heading, rather than solely in actuarial tables. We can no longer separate business and pensions: as the GE example shows, if pensions are compromised, so are businesses.

It's time for innovative change in how we run our futures: pensions can be a strategic part of creating incentive, growth, and value for our organizations.

3

ENVIRONMENT FOR RETIREMENT

CANADA'S POPULATION IS aging, like the populations of other Western countries. The last census in Canada, which took place in 2016, showed that there were 5.9 million people aged sixty-five and older in the country, which is the largest increase in that age group over prior demographic findings in almost a century.[1] By 2025, one in five Canadians will be sixty-five or older. As of 2020, the fertility rate is 1.60, which means we are not replacing ourselves.[2] What contributes to Canada's 0.88 per cent population growth are migrants who, hopefully, are prepared to enter the labour force.

This is because as the world's population increases, the rate of births is decreasing—especially in Canada and Europe. From an economic perspective, a rapidly aging population could have a detrimental impact on future generations. To secure our financial future, we need to take a fresh look at how the workforce is evolving as we bring new pension designs to light to help businesses succeed.

We need to look at how our aging society affects how we plan for our futures, whether or not we have a secure pension in place. Demographic movements could impact pension fund performance because generational shifts may affect new contributions, productivity, and growth. Despite the assumption that pension plans assure the elderly of a secure future, this is not necessarily the case.

In Canada, company pension plans are defined as any corporate savings plan that employees contribute to through their payroll, which can include matching plans, defined benefits, or RSP investment strategies, and which act as a benefit because of corporate co-investment. This separates corporate plans from Canada and Quebec Pension Plans (CPP/QPP), which are federally mandated investments to which every worker in Canada can contribute, as well as two other programs called Old Age Security and (for those with no other resources) the Guaranteed Income Supplement.

Despite the federal mandate, however, few Canadians are financially ready for retirement. A 2019 report from a CIBC poll suggests that 32 per cent of Canadians between forty-five and sixty-four have nothing saved for retirement, and 53 per cent of Canadians say they don't know if they are saving enough.[3] Out of those who have been saving, only 10 per cent of them have a plan in place.

This is despite the fact that, as CIBC estimates, the average Canadian needs at least $756,000 for our now-normal thirty years of retirement, and this is a very conservative estimate when we think about how inflation has affected growth indicators in recent years. The CIBC poll discovered that most people have saved only around $184,000 by the time that they retire. And we're not alone: Americans have an even worse savings rate in place, with the median amount of post-job savings hitting only US $5,000.

So, why is this the case? Why do we in the Western world, with all the resources we have at our fingertips, fail to plan ahead when we know that we're so far from our goals? In what ways are we lacking in this area, and what can we do to change things?

The social and economic context of aging

How many members of the working-age population are needed to support those over age sixty-five? More than we think.

CPP/QPP was set up originally as an investment in our future, rather than an investment in a fund: current workers are meant to provide the tax dollars needed to fund retired workers. For every individual who retires, there needs to be 2.3 people contributing to Canada pensions at the current replacement rate. As we age as a society, and more people retire, that number has been on the increase.

As a larger-than-ever-before proportion of Canadian society, namely, baby boomers, ages into retirement, we as a nation will face many challenges to support our elderly population that will complicate our ability to rely on CPP/QPP. In addition to being at risk of psychological, mental, and physical disabilities, which increase economic and social costs, the frail elderly population are vulnerable and lack economic support and, therefore, are unable to successfully mitigate the financial demands of old age. This means that the cost of being elderly may be going up for our social services: the more that we age as a society, the more that we need to pay for health care and other costs. Not only can the elderly not work, but more funds will be needed to pay for health care because older patients' illnesses and recovery cycles are likely to be much more complex than younger patients', and government benefits for seniors are likely to exceed the ability of the younger generations to pay for these services.

The predicament we are in is, however, a result of changing social norms around aging.

As a result of capitalism and neoliberalism, aging has come to be understood in terms of biological science's attention to innate and virtually immutable processes, in which the utility of the human being slows and then comes to an end.[4] A person who once was a thriving member of society becomes perceived as limited and useless because they are no longer able to contribute to their own or others' financial health. When a society holds, as one of its primary values, a focus on economic production and efficiency, the elderly are likely to suffer.

"Ageism" refers to the cultural, political, and socio-economic discrimination of people on the basis of age, but as noted in an article from CNN, ageism is not only imposed upon people but can also be internalized.[5] As people age and they believe that they will become infirm, there is a greater chance that they will. As noted in the article, at a recent meeting of the National Academies of Sciences, Engineering, and Medicine's Forum on Aging, Disability, and Independence, it was found that if aging people believed in their own ability to be well, they lived an average of seven and a half years longer than those who did not. The article suggests that the elderly need to combat their own biases against what it means to move through this part of the human development cycle so that they can have a happier and healthier time as older people.

The reality is, though, that when the elderly are affected by poverty, they won't necessarily be able to achieve this goal. With the current set-up of CPP/QPP, the average elderly person will receive just over $13,000 per year in benefits. It is thought by many that the federal government's plan cannot sustain itself. With fewer younger people contributing to the fund, the amount of subsidies available to the elderly in their retirement decreases. Not only will they not be able to lean on federal pensions, but also our social world has changed in a significant way so that fewer elderly people are living with their younger relatives.

And so, we're looking at how to integrate long-term care into our community and health care planning. In 2002, the Romanow report suggested that the current health care system, as it stood, could not support the Canadian public for an undefined period of time.[6] As noted by Romanow, with a rising average age, there would be more seniors in the country than ever before, placing a burden on the health care system because of their natural frailty, and an equal burden on the taxpayers of Canada to fund their care. There was, according to Romanow, a need for new infrastructure that would align with the health care demands of this population and with an increased number of immigrants to make up for the population deficit. The changes that he recommended included expanding long-term care facilities across the board. Ontario is already doing this: the province started creating budgets for long-term care in 2016 so that the elderly will have a place to live, given that there are so many constraints on their incomes in the present day.[7]

What do all these demographic changes mean for the average person edging towards retirement? What is the role of business, the government, and individuals retiring, or those preparing to become part of a new workforce? Will pensions still add value to business by attracting and retaining employees?

This changing social context is why so many people rely so heavily on investments to survive. In the table below, we can see how this has played out in the public sphere. The amount of RRSPs collected by Canadians in real dollars has increased in a massive way over the last twenty-five years. And these are not corporate pension plans; these funds, belonging to Canadians, are put aside to manage their own futures.

Pension savings combined: RRSPs collected per year (adjusted for inflation)

	1993	2003	2016
	$ thousands	$ thousands	$ thousands
Total accumulated RRSP assets	6,974,700	13,382,221	40,394,515

Source: Data from "Chart 18.6—Enlarged Version and Data Source," Statistics Canada, last modified July 7, 2007, https://www150.statcan.gc.ca/n1/pub/11-402-x/2007/3868/grafx/htm/ceb3868_003_6-eng.htm.

Even with this increase, Canadians, as mentioned, are not putting aside enough. In 2016, according to the data from Statistics Canada, only 23 per cent of people were putting money towards RRSPs, at a median rate of $3,000 per year.[8] In Canada, non-governmental pension plans account for almost sixteen times the wealth of CPP/QPP.

Financially, therefore, it could be assumed that people are relying on corporate pension funds. But are they?

The reality for workers

In today's corporate climate, a pension paid out after decades of work with the same firm is no longer guaranteed. The ways in which pensions are both designed and doled out are changing significantly.

As Statistics Canada reports, "Canadian firms... have responded to growing competition within industries and from abroad by reducing their wage offers for new employees, by offering temporary jobs to a growing proportion of them, and by offering less often pension plans that guarantee defined benefits at the time of retirement."[9] Not only are fewer companies offering pension plans to their employees, but they are redefining the work relationship as temporary or part time so that in cases where health care benefits are offered to full-time staff, workers are not eligible for them.

This means that the pension burden on the public sector, and on individuals themselves, may increase over time.

The answer for many companies and individuals are retirement funds, like RSPs, offered through banks and investment corporations. RSPs are made up of mutual funds—an amalgamation of high- to medium-risk stocks—combined with the safety net of government bonds. What does this mean for workers? That instead of a standard employment contract plus government pension to provide security in retirement, families from every walk of life now have to rely on the growth and sustainability of corporate investment to take care of them at the end of their lives.

At the same time, many companies are aiming to make the process of pension creation and management easier by giving employees stock options or company equity programs rather than true pensions. It is estimated that 20 per cent of the US labour force (22 million employees), for example, participate in over 400,000 workplace profit-sharing plans, and that the number of profit-sharing pension plans has increased by 19,000 per year since 1970.[10] Nonetheless, despite the fact that more conservative pension strategies based in mutual funds require substantially higher contribution rates for workers—therefore limiting their investment options outside their companies—equity-based strategies are much riskier over the long term for workers themselves.

Let's take a look at a case study that may help clarify this situation, to illustrate some of the challenges of changing economic influences such as shifts in demographics, and demonstrate why pension management is a key component of a company's human resource policies.

In 2005, Telus tried to merge several disparate collective pension agreements into a single long-term contract. This left Telus workers without a definitive contract for more than four years while the details were hammered out between management and representatives from the Telecommunications Workers Union. Thirteen thousand five hundred Telus workers in British Columbia and Alberta began job action to protest pension management standards in the merger between Telus and BC Tel, but were not able to return to work until October 23 of that year. In the interim, not only did Telus engage more than 5,000 management employees in front-line work to replace union staff, but also 50 per cent of union staff in Alberta crossed the picket lines. This ended up costing the company a significant amount of money as, over a number of years, processes were shifted to accommodate union action. Part of the reason for this dichotomy of workforce response was that employees in BC retained their existing BC Tel pensions when BC Tel was acquired by Telus; these workers were unwilling to negotiate the same deal as Albertan workers. The challenge was enormous: both the company and the union had to mitigate and merge the Telus and BC Tel pension contracts, along with employee and management expectations, to create a new comprehensive deal.

This example has been simplified, but it illustrates a fundamental disconnect in values between management and members. Company leaders often think about pensions as a nuisance and an expense. Workers count on them, though, to plan their futures at the same quality of life that they signed up for when they accepted their jobs. The impact of a nonchalant management attitude is profound when it comes to pensions. This case study shows that concerns over the viability of pensions can derail company operations if not managed correctly.

Many global externalities can affect the development and management of pension funds. Because more and more corporations are putting the onus on their employees to participate in choosing and managing the mutual funds that now make up the majority of their pensions, this must be accounted for on an ethical level. As pension researchers Mitchell and Utkus have written, "underlying this global movement spurring participant choice is an implicit assumption about behaviour: that the employee-citizen to whom the responsibility of choice has been handed is a well-informed economic agent who acts rationally to maximize his self interest."[11]

The end result for workers

Today's corporations are taking on more than just the role of inventor, manufacturer, or employer: they are subsuming yesterday's government by providing retirement support for most Canadians. Pensions are even subsuming the role of yesterday's family, as, in an increasingly independent society, they provide the kind of support that used to come from the social obligation to care for the elderly. To this end, government and corporate interests seem to intersect positively when it comes to providing retirement security for Canadians. When the risks of pension and retirement planning are absorbed by corporations and do not fall to tax revenues or families, the buck is well and truly passed.

But corporations cannot always accept this role. And that means that workers, especially low paid and precarious ones, may be more at risk than ever before.

The reality of poverty in Canada today is that much of it is hidden. We live in a country known for its prosperity and social support systems; most people assume the level of poverty in Canada is much lower than it is. As a result of this widespread assumption that people have access to assistance and are not comparatively poor, many people, and even communities, become invisible, and their basic needs are not met. There are pockets of endemic poverty in many areas of the country, and among certain socio-demographic groups that are left unchecked by society, policy makers, and leaders.

In fact, Canada has one of the highest poverty rates among member-countries of the Organisation for Economic

Co-operation and Development (OECD). One in six Canadians falls under the poverty line, which is a much higher level than expected, and many elderly face the risk of not having enough money upon which to retire.[12]

Existing welfare policies are a legacy rather than a reflection of our current reality. The welfare state was designed to serve what was known as the "deserving poor," namely, people who are too old or too young to work, people with disabilities, and those who are infirm. At the same time, the way in which poverty has been measured has changed over time, and at present there is contention as to what level of income represents poverty, and so many people end up slipping through the cracks.

Without a good income at retirement, the elderly may be subject to food and housing insecurity and barriers to social support systems, both those created through policies and those that arise naturally in a community, such as friendships, partnerships, and collegial support systems. This means that these individuals may face not only endemic economic barriers but also barriers to their personal security and health over the long term.

It will cost Canada more if these fundamental barriers to retirement security are not addressed. And, perhaps unexpectedly, it's also going to create risk for corporations.

Companies are a part of our communities, and poverty will affect their long-term sustainability. If we drive both workers and consumers to the lowest common denominator of pension choices, it's going to affect taxation, regulation, and employee morale.

Pension plans must be created in consideration of both immediate and potential future externalities, such as government regulations, macroeconomic shifts, and local and international accounting practices. Companies looking to create a viable pension plan need to develop the means to integrate new knowledge and adjust to external shifts over time so that the pension is not negatively affected in the long term. Pension managers need to understand not only the development of the company's own finances but also the ways in which external factors can affect the sustainability of the pension plan.

What does this mean for the design, management, and outlook of after-work pay? First, normally when we evaluate the sustainability of a pension fund, we make certain assumptions about growth, namely, that pension payments consist of 30 per cent from contribution and 70 per cent from investment returns. We need to be clear about what we expect to get from future returns on our investments, and consider whether conventional assumptions are sustainable. Second, if we need superior productivity from employees to generate economic output and encourage growth, we need to inspire people to be at their best so that their financial future is secure.

Do we need population growth to sustain economic growth, and can our financial and other resources, as they presently stand, support the kind of growth we're used to? Today, it looks like that ultimate limit is set by our natural resources and the sustainability of our environment, but what we've seen in this chapter is a call to action when it comes to our people.

To this end, organizations must create an ethical way to introduce their employees to financial management. Because employees may be unaware of their rights, and because they have proved to be overconfident in their financial-planning skills, companies must complete due diligence in ensuring that pension choices are understood by employees.

4

THE PSYCHOLOGY OF MONEY

THE USE OF and access to money has been said to change people's motivation and their behaviour towards others, both for the better and, more often, for the worse.[1] In fact, research shows that there may be a negative psychological impact in striving to accumulate wealth over the long term.[2] At the same time, research also shows that money can positively affect a person's level of happiness, albeit weakly.[3]

What is the relationship, then, between money psychology and a person's choices with respect to pensions? How can companies create optimal pension plans that motivate employees to perform? Why do people strive to get money and then hoard it or use it as a tool?

Everyone knows that money is often used as a carrot in business. This is especially true when it comes to thinking about the purpose behind pensions. The promise of a safe and secure future, as provided by a pension, is a carrot.

Although there are other short-term financial incentives, such as bonuses and stock options, pensions are the most common direct financial benefit offered to the average worker in the Western world.[4]

This means that most business leaders need to better understand how their employees think about money. This isn't as simple as providing more money or better pensions for employees. In fact, research from the field shows that most people are not directly incentivized by money, and creating the right solution is not as simple as creating job security or even financial stability for the average employee. Knowing how your employees think is not about getting them to save more money themselves, at least not directly. (We'll dig into this research in the next few pages.)

What does this mean for employee leadership, then? Are pensions really the incentive we have long believed them to be? And if not, what can we do about creating the right financial framework for our teams?

Knowing the psychology of money will help leaders understand their employees better and, therefore, better appreciate what it takes to create a secure future in the workplace.

Theory meets practice

Before we get to leadership and best practices, let's start with understanding just how the mind of the average person thinks about money.

A number of theories seek to explain our relationship with money on a psychological level and can enhance the way that we apply leadership frameworks in pension management. These psychosocial theories may shed some light on the ways in which people interact with money and other capital resources, and how companies can best use incentives to inspire engagement.

Expectancy theory of motivation

Motivation theory is linked to our earliest beliefs about money and work. And it's a theory you've probably heard about throughout your working life, in one way or another.

This theory suggests that people are motivated in relation to perceived rewards, especially money. The expectancy theory of motivation is closely aligned with Abraham Maslow's hierarchy of needs, and what he called self-actualization and peak experiences.[5] Essentially, every human being has to first meet their fundamental needs (food and shelter) before attempting to satisfy more sophisticated desires that relate to our higher reasoning, like self-actualization.

Money is the modern means by which fundamental needs are met.

An extension of this hierarchy is what is known as expectancy-value theory. This theory's guiding principle is that expectancy times value equals motivation.[6] In other words, to be motivated to complete a task, a person needs to experience both expectancy and value. For example, the task might be the time and effort it takes to bid on a project. The person assigns value to that work, such as how much money they deserve to make on an hourly basis on the job. Life experience also factors in. For example, a worker may decide that a job at a coffee shop is worthwhile for a wage of $11 per hour but not $10 per hour. Thus, the individual can decide on their level of motivation to complete the task based on the value of this money.

In a recent large-scale study about work and motivation in the United States, however, results of a poll of currently employed workers show that money may not be directly related to decisions about pensions and retirement. The strongest predictors for leaving a company were connected to employees' need for change, boredom, or feeling tired of working at a company, regardless of their pension plan or how many benefits they had accrued.[7]

Employee motivation, therefore, may not always be linked to positive incentives. But let's dig further.

Motivation-hygiene theory

Maslow's theory was only the first that looked in depth at motivation and external factors. Frederick Irving Herzberg, the developer of motivation-hygiene theory, was an American psychologist who became one of the most influential names in business management because he delved more deeply into how job satisfaction, job dissatisfaction, and motivation are connected. Herzberg showed business leaders that the task of motivating employees was a lot more complex than simply providing them with money and other benefits.

What he means by "hygiene," by the way, has nothing to do with keeping clean. It's about separating out the causes for satisfaction from dissatisfaction in the workplace. Herzberg demonstrated that these are two entirely different things, and that they are fundamentally unrelated to one another.

Let's start with what satisfies the average employee.

Factors that are likely to increase an individual's motivation include task achievement, recognition for achievement, intrinsic interest in the task, increased task responsibility, advancement, and the possibility of occupational growth, some of which can result in the acquisition of money. An increase in salary, or an increase in pension benefits, results in satisfaction because it is often also an indicator of a person's achievement on the job.

In essence, motivational factors result in financial growth for an individual.

Dissatisfaction factors may, however, be more important to motivation than those related to satisfaction, strangely enough.

Dissatisfaction factors can include the imposition on the worker of a company's administration and policy; supervision; working conditions; and limits on salary, status, job security, and interpersonal relationships, all of which might lead to either a lack of money or an increase in money security. All these factors are associated with pain avoidance linked to financial risk. The greater a person's financial risk, the greater the potential for upset. A definitive connection, therefore, can be observed between hygiene factors and psychological issues such as stress and depression in the workplace.

Field research in recent years, however, has shown that although there is a strong connection between motivation and happiness, financial strength in pension plans is *not* the key factor that leads to employee motivation.

The factors that *do* matter to employees planning for the future include clarity about retirement goals, the strength of financial goals, and an alignment between personal values and self-beliefs around their pensions.[8] In other words, linking employee motivation to the motivation-hygiene theory means creating a plan an individual can rely on and a goal that person can work towards, rather than providing an exceptional amount of money. Although every penny counts, what seems to count more is offering employees a sense of control over their future.

Self-determination theory

Given the need for personal control, self-determination theory may help reveal even more about the link between motivation and pensions.

This theory is grounded in the idea that the quality of motivation is more important than the quantity of motivation. Two primary types of motivation exist: autonomous and controlled motivation. Autonomous motivation involves recognizing the value of the activity itself; this value can be financial or personal. Controlled motivation involves external regulation, such as a supervisor at a job or a financial reward for performance, as well as the external influences that affect behaviour, like what's happening in the economy at any given time. It also includes the idea of interjected regulation, in which one's intrinsic motivation to complete a task is mediated by outside influences, such as approval from others or avoidance of negative consequences (the loss of money or punishment for doing a poor job, for example).

Self-determination theory shows that there is a social component to the psychology of money and its links to motivation. The idea of gaining approval from others or avoiding negative consequences can be connected to social network theory, which suggests that our ability to navigate social networks successfully may allow us to gain access to money. And we may feel positive or negative emotions based on our ability to achieve this goal. According to this theory, social events that support feelings of competence—such as an award for performance at a job, a contest, or an opportunity to display a specific skill—may be more important than money. Other social factors include freedom from negative evaluation as well as support for desirable challenges and constructive feedback that enhances performance.

Similar to motivation-hygiene theory, self-determination theory shows that the connection between financial success and motivation may be very indirect.

In fact, recent research into pension motivation shows that those who *are* more interested in money than in social reward are few and far between.[9] When self-gain is the fundamental motive, financial goal achievement becomes the focus. Money might foster a mindset of disregard of those who do not facilitate people's self-gain and goal achievement. In other words, if individuals are provided with only financial incentives, this may lead to poor teamwork at the office. Increasing social rewards in the workplace may offset employee demands for benefits or other financial incentives.

Downward social comparison theory

The psychology of money and its links to motivation may be connected to the psychological construct of downward social comparison.

Downward social comparison is the act of looking down on those who have a lower income or less social capital. Essentially, downward social comparison allows individuals to create a more positive mood and outlook on their own future because someone else is always worse off. This process is a defence against feelings of inadequacy or failure.

If people need proof of their financial achievement, then they will be moved to compare themselves with those who either do, or do not, reach the desired wealth. Likewise, if they are motivated to be seen as part of a collective group, such as a corporate department that includes high performers, they will perhaps be more likely to rate themselves against the goal of affiliation with that group. If people feel guilty about their own decisions or experiences in life, then knowing that others have experienced similar or worse situations, such as bankruptcy, is likely to decrease a sense of regret for their choices.

In essence, the process of downward social comparison makes it possible for individuals to forgive themselves for anything they have done to make their future insecure, or forgive themselves for the lack of financial success that they have achieved at work. By looking at others who have achieved less, some individuals feel better about themselves.

The core takeaway for leaders is that downward social comparison theory may explain why people may react unexpectedly when they find out that they have more (or less) money than their peers.

When people have access to money, they may distance themselves from those around them and be more likely to reject requests for assistance from people close to them.[10] When they have less money, they feel as if they have done something wrong.

There may be two psychological reasons for this. The first reason is that individuals with money may want to avoid the risk of not having it in the future and, therefore, develop a hoarder mentality that prevents them from sharing their wealth. The second reason is that downward social comparisons may result in an individual's negative perception of those around them, and may prompt the individual with money to unconsciously fear that if they share their money, the recipient of it may rise socially in comparison.

In other words, gaining access to money can become more *symbolic* than it is *practical*.

People need money to survive, but the way that people unconsciously consider the value of the money they do, or do not, have isn't always tied to survival. For leaders, therefore, it is vital to recognize that although money matters, what that money represents to people is more important.

What does all this mean?

From the point of view of pension leadership, the biggest takeaway from motivation theories and field research into pensions is that money is not everything.

Research into the psychology of money shows that our reliance on currency as an indicator of success and the focus of our lives' work is not necessarily healthy or effective. In fact, although money can positively affect a person's level of happiness and work effort, this is in a very limited way.

And so, creating a high-output pension plan should not be treated as the only objective, or even the most important objective, in helping employees plan for retirement.

Should leaders view pensions as a place of motivation?

Yes, but only insofar as pensions are, like money, symbols of what really matters. *A pension can be seen, more than anything, as a corporate endearment, but one that is critical to employee well-being.* Having a pension makes people feel safe, and having the same pension and benefits as everyone else makes people feel like they are at least as valuable as the person at the next desk. Not having a pension makes people feel at risk, because, as we've discussed in earlier chapters, the social context of money is changing, and people have fewer sources of retirement funds upon which they can rely.

What actually works?

Given these findings, when planning pensions, leaders need to focus on a few key standards of management that will build the right kind of incentive in the workplace.

Building monetary intelligence

As a recent international study suggests, business leaders ought to shift from a focus on financial pension planning to a focus on monetary intelligence for employees through active training.[11] Just as emotional intelligence is used to improve business relationships, monetary intelligence aims for a more nuanced understanding of economics and finance among team members in a business, so that they will make better decisions for their own financial futures as well as that of the company. The authors of this study suggest that workers will benefit from feeling as if they are stewards of their own financial choices, if they have the right knowledge to make choices that benefit them. Positive stewardship of money, they write, results in better coping behaviours when the status quo changes, as well as decreased avoidance of challenges that arise at work and at home. On the flip side, without monetary intelligence, people feel afraid for their futures, and this short-term financial mentality will affect their ability to make the right choices for themselves and the businesses in which they work.

Developing heterogeneity in pensions

Because financial incentives are secondary to personal values placed on money, we have to think about a range of strategic options for pensions. For example, research in the Netherlands has shown that replacing full-time pension schemes with schemes that offer gradual retirement opportunities induces workers to retire one year later, on average, and increases productivity and knowledge management in companies, especially for teams with workers who have lower than average wages.[12] In other words, creative pension planning can include a varying work and retirement schedule in which people can gradually increase their draw from their pension money and decrease their working hours.

Supporting equity and quality of life at work

Because people feel as if they are being constantly compared to each other at work, they may have difficulty with downward (or upward) social comparison. Employees need to know that they have the same options and benefits as others at work. This is where pensions, in being framed as standard for all employees, can serve to motivate employees in a way that sales bonuses or stock options, which are often reserved for certain work groups, cannot. As a result, leaders ought to regularly communicate the benefits of the pension plan, and use it as a key touchstone for employees to show how the business is supporting their future happiness and quality of life.

Employees need to be taught how to use, understand, or optimize their own pensions and learn how to plan for their life after retirement. They then have to be given the flexibility to use these skills and life choices on their own, so that they feel safe and secure.

Ultimately, if employees feel as if they have active choices in planning for their futures through self-determination, and as if they are receiving the same benefit as others, they are more likely to feel motivated in their work.

Let's break it down to brass tacks

All this means that pension managers would be best served by looking at how they can

- address employees' real retirement concerns and objectives, which include quality of life, equity, and feeling valued;

- develop monetary intelligence in their workforce through an active education plan so that people can definitively plan for their futures;
- support positive management styles so that the work itself, rather than employees' relationships with money, is the driving force in creating positive work outcomes; and
- build capacity for retirement planning at every level of the organization so people feel secure and satisfied.

Leaning in to monetary intelligence and flexibility in pension options will serve employees and the organization alike. It will allow for teams to negotiate better pension plans on both the management and employee sides of the table. It will create happier and more secure employees who feel prepared for every eventuality.

This approach is a positive leadership choice, rather than a financial choice, but it's also the right way to create alignment with the psychology of money.

That's because the true motivation equation is simply this: building purpose and quality of life into organizations, plus treating people as human beings who can't be bought by a lump sum, plus creating shared values while simultaneously delivering business results.

5

HOW ACTUARIES WORK, AND HOW LEADERS OUGHT TO WORK

"CANADIANS ARE LIVING longer than ever, and many are choosing to work beyond age sixty-five," John Dark, president of the Canadian Institute of Actuaries, recently stated. "It makes sense to update our country's retirement income programs to reflect this fact."[1]

In his statement on the future of pensions, Dark was suggesting that every pension strategy in Canada align with a simple idea: that we ought to push pension enrollment to a later date in life, with the Canada Pension Plan/Quebec Pension Plan deferring its benefits from the age of sixty-five to sixty-seven, and deferring Registered Retirement Saving Plan income payouts to seventy-five, instead of seventy-one.

Dark is right: we are living longer lives and many people are working long past "retirement age." That people will end their working life when they turn sixty-five, on the dot, is no longer a given.

At the same time, however, we have to understand that Dark's recommendations come from a specific point of view, namely, that of the actuarial profession. Is this set of estimates, and his associated recommendations, going to have the effect that he assumes it will? Or is Dark advising policies from within the silo of his professional knowledge?

Actuaries are number crunchers, and they're wonderful at it. Their aim is to predict what might happen in the future based on statistical analysis of data: retirement age, termination rate, life expectancy, and lots of other factors affect how we currently determine pension frameworks and plans.

Most of the time their numbers are helpful, but there are gaps between what we believe actuarial numbers tell us and what we need to understand in the context of business. We need clarity on whether conventional actuarial methods impact the way we need them to.

Pension design should not be focused on running the numbers to avoid risk. That just drives up the billable hours of actuaries, without making substantive positive changes. To be an informed leader, do you have to understand economics, actuarial science, and mathematical calculations? Is their analysis helpful to decision making? Are actuarial tables the most important component of business decisions on pensions? Will actuarial recommendations result in the right outcomes for Canadians?

Pension management needs more transparency, not more actuaries crunching more numbers. It's not about being a financial hero but about making things happen that work for *your* organization.

It's all about the numbers

Many organizational leaders are dissatisfied with the current limitations of risk management practices, and pensions are not exempt from this.

When actuaries come to the table armed with reams of data, it helps people in leadership positions feel confident that they are going to do the right thing. Everyone is constantly looking for more accurate calculations, more precise mortality projections, more precise assumptions about demographic changes, and with today's technology, we can go deep adding precise science to the mix, almost every step of the way.

That's why many business leaders rely on actuaries to provide them with best-case scenarios for pension management.

One of the problems, however, is that even with the best of intentions and mathematical prowess, we cannot always work in a way that protects pensions over the course of generations. Actuarial tables seem to present us with a solution based on quantitative science, so we sometimes don't step back and look at all the other factors that will affect pensions over the long term, which can put us at risk.

It's a complex issue that we will to dig into, but the truth is that the search for accuracy in numbers sometimes clouds our human judgement and intuition. Sometimes, we are better off being approximately right than precisely wrong.

What is pension risk management, really?

Actuaries are perceived as the primary key to insuring against pension risks. When it comes to pensions, risks are grouped into two categories, namely, defined contribution (DC) and defined benefits (DB) plans.

In DC plans, all plan members (and sometimes their employer) pay into an account each month. These contributions are used to purchase assets, such as mutual funds or some other asset. At retirement, these assets can be withdrawn. This means that the risks associated with DC plans are linked to the performance of the asset: if the company provides limited choices for assets, such as only stock options (which may be non-performing), or the employee chooses the wrong asset in a large list of possible assets (for example, a selection of mutual funds), then that employee's pension earnings may be negligible.

Internal and external factors, therefore, can lead to DC plan risks for those receiving the pension; but employers using this kind of pension also may, in some cases, bear an ethical risk with respect to their responsibility to employees. Relying on the market alone to ensure that an employee has a pension burdens the employee with understanding their options and the associated risks.

In DB plans, employers use formulas that usually depend on the number of years worked and salary to calculate a fixed pension amount to pay the employee upon retirement.

The risks associated with DB plans are linked to internal factors more than external ones. The risk of varying rates of return of pension assets falls on the employer—its leadership team and its internal financial management. This risk affects wages, as well as shareholders and customers.[2]

In order to mitigate DB risks, organizations need a lot of cash assets on hand. Compliance with all government regulations is required. Structural risk assessment protocols and internal stress testing has to take place. Recent economic, market, and peer institution stresses must be brought into each equation.

That's a lot of work.

Theoretically, risk analysis of pensions is much simpler than it is for, say, insurance provision, which also relies heavily on actuarial information. In insurance, risk assessment is based on imperfect random population data, and you need to build in profit factors for the insurers to make money, both of which skew any data analysis of risk.

For pensions, the numbers are much more predictable, since determining when people will retire, for example, is quite simple.

A firm can follow a risk-based approach and rely on actuaries to try to churn the numbers in the right way to make decisions.

But here's the challenge.

Actuarial tables are based on aggregate numbers and aren't necessarily predicting risk in a way that helps. What are aggregate numbers? They are facts about a large-scale group of people. We don't complete an actuarial analysis on every single human being on the planet. Aggregate figures might tell us that 20 per cent of people in Canada are likely to save 10 per cent of their income every month in a savings account, but is this true for an individual working at a pharmacy in Orillia? Not necessarily. We group people together and predict based on what we assume they will do, based on our past experience with employee patterns.

But what we get are probabilities, not facts.

When business leaders see the precise numbers that actuaries put on tables, they sometimes take it as a given that these *are* facts. That nothing will ever go wrong. But we tend to forget that actuarial valuations are only estimates, a snapshot of a scenario to be used as a guide, not a precise measurement of what is to come.

Just as an engineer designing a bridge needs to consider what would happen in the case of an earthquake rather than just what happens during the average rush hour, pension managers also need to consider the likelihood and possible effects of a large-scale event getting in the way of perfect predictions. For example, when companies go bankrupt, or economies melt down, as they did in 2008, we are reminded that some risks are truly unpredictable. We never know when double digit inflation is going to hit, which no one wants to pay for. There is a conflict between different parties, namely, managers past and present, neither of whom wants to pay for a possible future risk.

Here's an example.

In some current DB plans, actuarial recommendations provide a specific dollar figure for the maximum contribution to a plan. Let's pretend that dollar figure is $100 per employee per month. Some employers assume that if they contribute that $100 recommended by the actuary, then the plan will be fully funded. What the employer is unlikely to factor into their decision-making process is that if they contribute $100, there is an *85 per cent probability* that the plan will become fully funded *in fifty years*. The timeline and the level of risk are totally misunderstood.

This kind of thinking has led to some expensive lessons in pension conversions, some of which have tossed out DB plans altogether, only to have to reconvert to DB later, after business leaders found out the effects of these choices.

Fighting the risks, the right way

So, how does a business leader find the right information to choose the right pension?

In their fascinating book, *The Tyranny of Uncertainty*, Nabil Abu el Ata and Rudolf Schmandt, both global experts on risk management for banking systems, write:

> The Greek philosopher Heraclitus said, "No man ever steps in the same river twice, for it's not the same river and he's not the same man." But we continue to treat risk with a static and closed view of systems. We ignore the hidden influences that may be formed by design or through environmental factors, as well as those caused by changes in the dynamic system over its lifetime. *We pretend that our perception of risk is objective, remains constant, and unaffected by human dynamics* [emphasis added]. And so we are surprised when dynamic complexity suddenly causes a risk to appear.[3]

Given what we know about pension management, Abu el Ata and Schmandt are entirely correct. John C. Bogle, who died in 2019, was a career investor credited with creating the first index fund, and a major philanthropist. He stated, "I think we give far more credence to past returns in the stock market than they even remotely deserve. The past is not prologue. The stock market is not an actuarial table. As has been mentioned, and John Maynard Keynes told us back in 1936—and I put a lot of numbers on this—it's the sources of the returns... that determine future returns, not the recurrence of an ongoing event that comes up on a standard probability distribution curve."

What did Bogle mean when he claimed this? And why does it matter? He pinpointed the key difference between actuarial science and DC pensions in particular, but really, he's shown us the essential flaw in our human logic. We want to believe that we can predict the future, but as his long life in the market proved to him, we cannot do that. Although the market may be the most efficient place to put our money, institutional investments can be challenging to create and maintain.

Business leaders have to start with the assumption that they are not going to be able to predict the future, no matter how much information they have, and no matter how convinced their actuarial experts are that the data they have collected is correct. That data is probably correct, but there are limitations on how it can work. Aggregate numbers will provide somewhat accurate probability, but they don't work all the time.

So, is actuarial work for pensions becoming obsolete? No.

We need to bring actuarial work to light. Actuarial thinking is the key to pension resilience, but we may need to use unconventional methods to get to the heart of the data and use it in the right way. What we need to know is that the data actuaries collect and use is not always the be-all and end-all of our decision-making process.

Let's take a look at why this is the case.

With medical science and big data, we may be able to better pinpoint individual mortality, and, therefore, what the optimal age of retirement should be, but we still need to take this data with a grain of salt. Why is this the case? Actuaries use, as the foundation for their work, something called the Lee-Carter model of mortality. It is an algorithmic matrix of age-specific mortality rates ordered monotonically by time, and it has been used since the 1990s as the primary means to calculate the lifespan of a human being. In 2010, however, mathematical research showed that the trend can change over time, in particular because of various medical and social progresses, but perhaps even more importantly, *the algorithm is inaccurate when medical and social changes help people at or over the age of retirement.*[4] In other words, if people retired from Company X are sixty-five or older, and a medical breakthrough happens in cardiac health care, then those people are more likely to decrease their immediate risk of death than people who are younger. For pension managers, this is important, especially in the case of DB schemes, but it's also important for all people who face future retirement: all of a sudden the actuarial tables upon which companies made decisions, say, thirty years ago are completely inapplicable to their retired workforce. As a result, Company X may end up paying out retirement benefits for an extra ten years to a significant portion of its workforce.

Given this kind of disconnect, even within actuarial science itself, how can leaders in business use actuarial data productively?

- **Use techniques of asset liability management.** Findings from the field suggest that companies "need to make sure they will have a sufficient asset inflow to be able to make the future defined payments, in many cases with decades of uncertainty between the initial agreement and the actual payment of employee benefits. Fund managers need then to choose from a number of existing techniques, such as gap analysis, cash flow matching, standard immunization or portfolio insurance."[5] In other words, it's important to manage pensions in the same way that you manage other assets: through constant risk management techniques. This is only a start, however; there are flaws in some of these processes that are akin to those in actuarial analysis.
- **Support open resource sharing in business and actuary work.** Assessing high-risk impact issues, such as timelines and market forces, has to be achieved collaboratively in

order to be useful to pension planning. Companies need to learn from each other not after a pension has failed but as it is evolving. For example, the Colleges of Applied Arts and Technology (CAAT) Pension Plan in Ontario calls for the kind of governance that helps all parties evaluate the risk, so that there is no "too big to fail" thinking.[6]

- **Suggest different risk assessments for different data sets.** Research in the field shows that probability distributions of different risks can have different forms. Some risks are linear, others are barrier-like, others are logistical; as a result, not all risks can be presented by a single numerical estimate.[7] Exponentially growing risks are linked to new technologies such as AI or medical technologies such as nanosurgery, and may not be presented by a single annual probability. Leaders have to dig deeper than data to assess when, where, and how risks may affect their pensions.
- **Develop an internal mandate for corporate social responsibility that balances actuarial findings with employee engagement.** Partnership with employees needs to become fundamental to the examination of how to sustain pensions; this is a matter of risk management when a broad range of social norms need to be taken into consideration. Also, creating a focus on corporate social responsibility, such as training programs for employees to learn how to make informed choices about retirement, will allow firms to adapt more readily to shifts in the social

and economic space. An ethical company is one that can and will decide between right and wrong rather than between success and failure.

- **Hold actuaries to account.** Pension actuaries hold particular knowledge and experience that are key to pension development and innovation, but they need to step up as risk managers and be accountable for results in collaboration with the industry—with lawyers, investment managers, accountants, and most importantly, the real pension market, namely, the businesses that sponsor pension plans. Actuaries need to apply knowledge of business, economy, law, finance, and accounting and become experts in understanding their clients' interests and needs; they need to know what their clients can and cannot afford before anything happens, to quantify, guide, and manage unexpected events.

Actuarial analysis is more important than numbers

It is always the unknowns that impact performance: true resilience comes from managing the unexpected. The essence and art of actuarial science does exactly that. But that's not how conventional valuations have been regularly understood and used in today's pension market, or in boardrooms.

Actuaries do a pretty good job at analyzing mortality and demographic movements. But when it comes to predicting market performance and viability over the long term, conventional methods tend to fail more often than not.

This is where leadership is important. *It's a leader's job to ask questions.*

Businesses need to sort out the data itself from *what to do with the data*. This means that we may need a better pension planning model to build randomness into the process, accounting for real-life common sense and human experience, as well as the foibles of human nature. It is difficult to do this, however, when actuaries seem to speak a "foreign" language. But a leader can bring the conversation back to risk, market performance, and viability over the long term to shift the focus of the work. We truly need to worry about the compounding interest, the rate of returns, and the inflationary spiral, rather than only predictions about when people are likely to retire.

The goal of pensions is to help people and their spouses achieve financial security in their old age. But can an organization afford it? If actuaries think that the harsh actuarial reality is in conflict with management interests, who will stand up to explain exactly how expensive such a commitment is? It doesn't matter whether it is a DC or DB plan; we need to understand the true actuarial cost of financial need in retirement and act accordingly.

Pensions used to start with companies themselves, rather than actuaries, and we have to get back to that model. GM's president revolutionized investment management for pensions in the 1950s, and Procter and Gamble started the first pension program in the 1920s, before the first pension actuary ever existed. Although we're still looking for better ways to assess risk, leaders have to be the first point of call when it comes to decision making, and it's important to explore all the possible internal and external factors that are specific to your industry and company, and that may affect your pension outcomes.

There is no direct way to avoid the changes that we are currently undertaking as a society; our economic, social, and political boundaries are shifting in a large-scale and significant way. We need to imagine a different future for pensions, one in which we agree on what is important so that we can mitigate risk and keep our employees, our companies, and our global society safe and secure. We need clear thinking about market forces and how they affect pensions and businesses.

If we are to truly lead in pension management, then we need to create, implement, and adapt to a new way of thinking about our futures.

6

LEVERAGING THE LAW, FOR WORSE OR FOR BETTER?

REGULATIONS AND PENSION rules are meant to safeguard the pension system to ensure employers' and employees' money is looked after diligently, but even when companies follow the rules, they don't always pay attention to the details.

In Canada, the Wage Earner Protection Program (WEPP) provides for the payment of outstanding eligible wages to individuals whose employer is bankrupt or subject to a receivership. It's the last port of call for workers who ought to have received a pension, paying out a maximum of $7,150. There is, however, no legal guarantee to an individual receiving their pension from a company if that company collapses.

The same is true for the public sector. As Elizabeth Shilton's book *Empty Promises*—which investigates the legal tenets of pensions in Canada—suggests as well, even government and non-profit employers have taken up pension restructuring as a key strategy for managing the impact of austerity budgets and revenue losses. This is achieved through legal finagling that often leaves both workers and organizational leaders worse off over the long term.[1] Some company leaders, Shilton explains, have concluded that they ought to step out of pension provision altogether, leaving retirement savings up to their employees to manage on their own. But as we saw, this isn't necessarily in the best interests of companies, and it certainly isn't in the best interest of the economy: in a market economy like ours, changes in what we know as the nuclear family and the extended family mean that many of the most vulnerable in our society aren't getting the support they need in old age, which actually creates *more* of a financial burden for families.[2] This, in turn, puts pressure on the government and on taxation to provide for our elders, and it decreases consumer spending in other areas. Cutting out pensions is not a solution that's going to help build our economy, or our business community, then.

So how can pension managers use the law to create best practice frameworks for pension strategies?

Pension rules and actuarial science need to be followed with diligent care to ensure pension success. In this chapter, we'll look at why the law is challenging to navigate when it comes to pension management, but why shifting towards leadership allows businesses to leverage the law in a positive way. At the same time, while some lawyers who think in business terms have helped their clients greatly in making good decisions, this isn't always the case. How can we best use the law to create hope for our collective futures? We'll explore why business leaders need to create their own sustainable pension plans, relying on their own ideals and values.

The current legal standards

The Supreme Court of Canada set the most recent standard for employment pension trusts in 1994, in a case known as *Schmidt v. Air Products*. Air Products, a world-leading industrial gases company based in Canada, merged two defined benefit pension plans as a means to decrease administration costs and simplify work around pension management. The merger created a surplus that the company claimed it was entitled to. The plan members, however, decided to take Air Products to court, arguing that they were the ones who were entitled to the surplus. The court ruled against Air Products and stated that the creation of a pension plan constitutes a public trust, wherein there is a deep responsibility to the employees who have created the means by which the funds were collected in the first place, even if the employer contributes to those funds. Where surplus is part of the trust, therefore, the court set the standard that the employer will be entitled to it only if three standards are met:

- the employer was made a beneficiary of the trust from the outset;
- the employer reserved a power to revoke the trust when it was established; or
- something known as the doctrine of the resulting trust, namely, the presence of an implied trust between the organization and its employees, which naturally aims to support the weaker party, is applicable.

In this way, the court has tried to ensure that employees are protected from employer self-interest, especially given their deep pockets in comparison to the resources and power that the average employee has. As noted by researchers, employers sometimes use and hoard excess cash flows, including pension monies, to shore up the business rather than its pension plan members because returns earned on pension plan assets may be more attractive than other investment opportunities, leading to more investment in pension plans.[3]

This is the case because, for most people, there are two basic benefits of a pension: it is a mandatory savings plan that forces them to save for retirement, and there is a governance framework in place that requires pension committees to diligently review investment performance, which means that the pension is likely to be safe.

However, it's a little more complicated than that.

Pension plan assets do have the scale and ability to access certain investments (for example, private equities) that an individual may not be able to or only at a much greater cost. But that doesn't guarantee a greater return. Although this is not necessarily always a bad thing, it isn't always truly *legal*, given the standards of the court.

This may be why the promise of the *Schmidt v. Air Products* ruling, as Shilton explains, has not had the effects that the court may have imagined. As she writes:

> Since *Schmidt*, the Court has moved away from a conception of trust law as a fetter on employer power towards a flexible conception in which employer trust obligations are defined almost entirely by the terms of pension documents which those employers have themselves drafted. In the hands of Canadian courts, trust law has failed to operate as an independent source of rights for plan beneficiaries; instead, it has empowered employers to frame and administer plans in accordance with their own interests, even when those interests conflict with those of employee plan members. The Court's approach reflects its belief that employer control of pension plans and pension rights is fundamental to the survival of a voluntary employment pension system.[4]

In other words, the impetus of the court to protect the rights of employees has incentivized companies to create *different* pension plans, such as the move away from DB plans towards DC and RRSP plans, so that their responsibility towards employees is lessened. This may be upholding the letter of the law, but not the intention of it.

Does this mean that companies are in the clear legally? The answer, according to researchers and legal scholars, is no.

Pensions used to generate record returns in the stock market and, therefore, companies had the ability to play with surplus funds. Employers were putting extra money in pension funds for tax-free returns. Now, as a result of this kind of legal precedent as well as the demographic and economic changes in our midst, a lot has shifted. Most plans are in huge deficit, and it's the opposite issue that employers are concerned about: that they will be asked to put in more money while they struggle to even put in their minimum required contributions.

And, as the legal literature suggests, when there is a perceived hardship, many companies will look for loopholes that may or may not be fully legal.

Legality and justice

All components of traditional forms of law are, according to scholars, likely to be based on what is known as rational choice theory.[5]

Rational choice theory posits that citizens or corporate leaders will think through an underlying rational process before deciding on their best course of action, which will either increase their success or reduce their risk. The rational choice can be focused on either short-term or long-term goals, but the end result is that people will choose to help themselves in whatever way seems the most rational. A court's job is to mitigate the instances in which people act irrationally.

The fundamental problem presented in *Schmidt*, and the reason for the court's intervention, is that corporations rarely act according to rational choice, or at least they limit their rationality to specific parameters, such as those decisions that create access to capital. This is not a long-term, sustainable approach, as *Schmidt* states, because companies that do not act in the public trust will alienate not only their employees but also their customers.

The American poet Archibald MacLeish once said that the purpose of the law is not only justice but also to make sense of the confusion of life, so that we might reduce it to a place of order and give it possibility, scope, and essential human dignity.[6] Over time, companies must recognize that the legal, policy, and economic issues associated with pension provision, care, and dignity in old age are fundamental challenges for the future of our society and, therefore, for the future of their survival and success.[7]

That's why the law, when it comes to governance of corporate pensions, is shifting towards new definitions of responsibility linked to justice. This means that there is a difference between a focus on the law and a focus on justice.

Under the law, employers have considerable discretion and control in pension design and administration. Under new standards of social justice, pensions will likely need to respond to the changing workplace and the shift in our global demographics, and, in this way, directly address the needs and interests of those who are retiring.

The rise of generational fairness standards

Generational fairness should be a key part of how pension leaders negotiate legal pension terms in the coming years. As we've discussed in previous chapters, we're at a point in history at which more people are retiring than moving into the employment market.

People who have worked traditional full-time jobs and are currently in the process of retiring are putting pressure on funds originally designed for a much higher level of employee input over the course of generations. As we've discussed before, this has put many DB plans at risk, forcing companies to react quickly and sometimes failing on a spectacular level. Generational fairness suggests that there is a need to ensure that newer employees are not over-investing in their funds only for generations retiring before them to benefit more than they themselves ever will.

But there is, perhaps, an even greater cascade of risks that can affect pensions on a number of different levels.

At the heart of this question is asset and liability mismatch, states the literature on the subject, which leads to increased risk.[8]

The issue is whether the assets held are too volatile for the time profile of payments, thus generating excessive risk especially for members about to retire (assuming pension payments have priority). Alternatively, the fund may have shorter maturity assets than liabilities, giving rise to reinvestment risk. Fair value accounting has made for greater volatility of balance sheets as a result of mismatch. Deficits might give rise to a search for excessive yield to make up losses caused by mismatch, leading to credit risk. The result of this is that, in many countries, governments are imposing new pension regulations on corporations to curtail leadership decisions that ensure companies work under the letter of the law but not in alignment with fundamental justice—and the kind of trust that the Supreme Court of Canada has envisioned.

This effect is only beginning to take place, but corporate leaders ought to expect more regulations. More and more, lawyers state, international standards of social security set by the International Labour Organisation (ILO) and the Council of Europe will affect the pension processes of multinationals and trickle down to smaller businesses.[9]

Leadership and fiduciary duty

Businesses have to show real leadership in creating the right pensions based on a commitment to public trust, or they can be legally liable.

For Canadians, these changes are showing up in our courts in a set of decisions that suggest that companies owe a fiduciary duty to pension plan members and beneficiaries to *act in their best interests*, knowing that the pension is the de facto property of the plan members, not the company.[10]

But acting in the best interests of plan members is a complex challenge. Managers, as agents of the shareholders in a company, have a fiduciary duty to use corporate resources to maximize profit. There are flaws in this, however, from a legal point of view, as both employees and communities have an arguably larger "investment" in the firm, even if it is indirect or not financial. As agents of the company, managers have wide discretion to pursue a range of ends, and must recognize that, in terms of principles, shareholders may want more than profit maximization.

This is where corporate social responsibility (CSR) comes into play.

There are three generally accepted principles of CSR, which include economic security, human and labour rights, and environmental preservation. As noted in the literature, however, CSR can take many different forms.[11] Even though the notion of CSR has been around since the 1970s in business, its conceptualization is still unclear.[12] This is because, as Milton Friedman once argued, the role of a business was believed to be to generate profit, so that more people would be employed and, therefore, more of society would be secure. What we have seen since the 1970s is that a laissez-faire attitude towards CSR has resulted in all manner of business-led social failures, from the rampant overuse of resources to sweatshops to, as we are now seeing with clarity, challenges with pension management.

To this end, modern definitions of CSR are linked to the idea of value creation rather than profitability.[13]

For instance, the implementation of labour rights—which require companies to pay their workers fair wages, or provide them with a sustainable, trustworthy pension—directly affects the economy of the countries in which they work. The more that companies adhere to these standards, the higher the quality of life for more people and the more likely that those people will become or be maintained as consumers. Socially, upholding the human right to work without the fear of aging out of the workforce is pertinent to CSR and to the firm itself, because people cannot be productive and serve the company's interests if they are prevented from feeling confident and supported at work.

All in all, the overarching aims of building societal welfare can make corporations more successful as well. This means that, from a legal perspective, companies that use CSR are those that move one step further than what is generally required by the law. For example, the European Economic Commission defines CSR "as a template used by corporations—on a strictly voluntary basis, moving beyond mere compliance with legal requirements and market expectations—in order to integrate various social issues, environmental concerns, and stakeholder interest."[14] The law does not necessarily affect CSR viability, but if there is a clear breach, then the law will intervene. Companies can, in this way, operate within the law without having a clear and implemented CSR plan in place; and so there are still many grey areas in which companies may choose to modify their activities, either to feed their perceived need for profits or to engage in positive and long-term thinking about their broader role in society over the course of their market involvement.[15]

The impact of corporations on human rights is, even so, critical to the way in which people are protected at work and in the community. This impact has increased as the economic and political power of corporations has grown. In recent years, corporations have been called out to become more respectable as corporate citizens, which includes respecting the human rights of those affected by the corporation's actions, especially as we see the degradation of pensions coming to light in the Canadian legal system in cases such as Sears.

At the same time, however, corporate leaders are often deeply unaware of the ways in which these challenges are taking place, and how their decisions are affecting the community and the economy in ways that increase risk. In fact, in a study of whether companies have a legal and fiduciary duty to consider human rights, it was found that "the complex realities facing corporate decision makers will often necessitate making decisions that have potential impacts on many stakeholders including employees, consumers, suppliers, debt holders, option holders, governments, business partners, and local communities."[16] By placing the focus on one kind of fiduciary duty over another, this risk increases. Even though company leaders seem to think that ignoring fundamental justice issues is an informed risk they are willing to take, this is clearly an emerging issue.

Balancing the risk, making the ethical choice

All of this means that, for those running businesses, leadership decisions need to incorporate new definitions of fiduciary duty and the public trust, accounting for both local and global ideals, even if the company is nowhere near insolvency.

The standards are changing, and true leaders will become aware of how they can take a role in making things right. They will allow changes to take place so that the ideal of fundamental justice is embodied in their pension planning strategies. In a world of rapid change, of course, this means that pensions have to be flexible. It may be difficult to create a plan that aligns with the DB standards of the 1950s, for example.

But there is room for creativity.

The law says that company leaders need to balance the role of an employer and the role of an administrator with respect to a pension plan. This means that leaders have to make some serious decisions to resolve potential conflicts of interests and to build positive outcomes for their pension plans. Employers can begin with a few key approaches:

- **Be transparent.** Be clear about what you want to achieve and how you are going to see your pension plan through over time. For example, Ontario's risk-based regulatory framework, a program of proactive monitoring of pension plans and updating systems to detect plans at risk, provides hope for the future. This approach focuses on providing transparency above everything else, to protect employees and their pension plans and to provide clarity to businesses about what is expected and how they can be supported. Who is responsible for the design, implementation, funding, and monitoring of the plan? Who is responsible for creating member learning programs?

- **Combine different pensions.** The OECD has suggested that making pensions more sustainable means looking at a variety of options and bringing them together, through either employee choices or a varying-source portfolio. Combining funded and pay-as-you-go pensions, automatic mechanisms, and a strong safety net for pensioners improves retirement outcomes. What activities will be required to make the plan work? What are we already capable of doing given current resources?
- **Consider (and critically assess) shared investment options.** The law both in Canada and in other nations is changing to give pensions more flexibility in terms of where they are housed to promote long-term, sustainable pension design for employers and employees. But some flexible plans need critical thinking before implementation. The CAAT Pension Plan allows private employers to join this shared-risk plan, and some employers may find this easier and more flexible for their workplaces. But how big can it grow, and how will the plan sustain its returns?
- **Increase employees' knowledge of their pensions and of the law.** We have recommended this before, but it bears repeating. Financial education can result in better retirement outcomes, given that low levels of financial knowledge

and behavioural biases can lead people to make unsuitable decisions for retirement, but the law is increasingly asking employers to take employee education seriously.

- **Become your own devil's advocate.** In some regions, such as the UK, tools and training for pension trustees are readily available, but the same is not true here in Canada. Carefully consider and get a legal or consulting opinion on your risks and what to do when the future does not happen as expected. Do this ahead of the game so that you're always prepared to defend your position. Self-criticism will help you create the right checks and balances going forward. How are you evaluating your plan? Are there multiple ways? What's still needed—member guidance on governance, ongoing stakeholder engagement, quality tracking, cost metrics, communication effectiveness?

7

UNIONS, CHANGE, AND COLLABORATION

ONE OF THE foremost challenges in creating a retirement management plan that works is mitigating the needs of different stakeholders. The stakeholders with the largest number of people, especially for public organizations and manufacturing businesses, are often unions.

As this book is being written, in 2020, the Canadian federal government is facing this challenge, and a protracted, year-long battle with the Public Service Alliance of Canada's Customs and Immigration Union over pensions has yet to result in a solution. The union wants its members to be able to retire without a pension penalty after twenty-five years of service if they so choose.[1] The government disagrees, in part because they want to nudge people to stay longer in the workforce due to our present-day labour market economics, and in part because this long-established plan was set up to provide a very specific, and employee-beneficial, set of vestment standards. "Our understanding with the bargaining process is they're not even prepared to entertain that demand and that's the number-one demand," says Jean-Pierre Fortin, the union's national president. "I'm looking at where things are moving and it seems the government is pushing our members to escalate this and we're certainly prepared to fight for this."[2]

Why are both sides so entrenched in their positions, and why does it look like it will be impossible for negotiations to result in a positive outcome for anyone?

As of this writing, an outcome is yet to be seen for this particular case. The reality is, however, that unions are powerful stakeholders who represent the interests of many employees, which means that they have a lot of leverage and may take contentious action when pushed to their limits. Business leaders are also powerful stakeholders with a range of interests.

In this chapter, we will explore understanding businesses as human, social entities in which people often align with factions rather than negotiate win-win solutions. We'll talk about managing union relationships with pensions in mind, and developing shared-knowledge strategies well before pension negotiations take place. Finally, we'll discuss how to create new expectations and standards with unions, based on evidence from real-life case studies.

Businesses as human, social entities

A company's equity is, in part, driven by the value it creates in its people. To build and maintain product demand, the company has to rely on human resources, which means that the value of the company is embedded in each individual as well as the social structure of the firm. All companies and organizations have a financial responsibility. That's why employees and their needs have to be part of the discussion, and the research literature backs this up.

Let's start with this: most business factors that affect performance are embedded in the social structure of the organization as a whole, rather than in one individual or unit.[3] A goal of leadership in a company, among other things, is to create an effective social structure that will facilitate positive outcomes.

Social exchange theory suggests that there is a benefit to approaching work from the point of view of how people communicate and connect and, therefore, how they will act in the interests of the team rather than in their own interests alone.[4] In the creation of social networks in the firm, within units and across organizational levels, alliances that will result in best-practice integration can be formed. When team members understand their own role in protecting the interests of others, as well as the firm, this increases planning successes, decreases turnover, and results in more efficient, effective, and personally satisfied working groups throughout the firm.[5]

Every organization has its own unique social system, and even though it may be difficult to say whether there is one best style of management in any industry, managers are most effective in facilitating positive behaviour and compliance to strategic aims under certain conditions. One study of job satisfaction, employee engagement, and turnover at the Harvard School of Public Health found that managers are more likely to be productive at work "when they share a sense of mission (i.e. inspirational motivation), provide mentoring or coaching (i.e. individualized consideration), arouse employees to think in new ways (i.e. intellectual stimulations), and gain their employees' trust and confidence (i.e. idealized influence)."[6] Ultimately, this means that employees are psychological beings with needs that have to be met for their output to remain high.

In other words, social factors and individual psychological factors are going to be a part of the equation whether or not a company's leaders want to admit that they are.

Managing union relationships

Managing union relationships is no different from managing other corporate relationships. There is a need for commitment and involvement when it comes to day-to-day collaboration and for communication when it comes to pensions. Union members and leaders also need to be recognized and seen for what is important to them.

Let's go back to the example of the Public Service Alliance of Canada union. This is not just a matter of two stakeholders at odds. What exactly are they saying when they demand the ability to retire without a pension penalty after twenty-five years of service? What Fortin is asking for is related to union members' personal life choices. Not every employee is going to want to follow the same path and, as we know, people aren't on the same employment trajectory now as they were in the past. People don't start working at twenty-two only to retire at sixty from the same company or organization. Some members of Fortin's union may start working for the government when they are forty-five, which, of course, means that we're not talking about early retirement in some cases. Fortin doesn't want these individuals to be penalized based on their personal life choices or age. That may feel like a reasonable expectation for Fortin and his union to have. This is not to say that government leaders, or company leaders in similar positions, shouldn't be able to state their case or also present their own reasonable expectations.

But with the demographics of work changing, there is a need to look at more flexible pension plans that make sense for people's lives and retirement plans.

For example, mortality assumptions have changed since the Public Service Alliance plan was envisioned, and the cost may be even higher now because we are living longer. What pension factors, then, are most relevant to members? Which pension is the best for workplace management and to ensure the best service outcomes? Can there be a phased retirement program in which people have choices that would benefit both the members and the public, such as moving to a part-time job later in their career while still contributing to the company pension?

Successful management of union relationships involves paying attention to details and ensuring that everyone, including those inside and outside the management team, has the tools that they need to connect and engage in creating a culture aligned with pension planning excellence. It means looking at the human, social entity of work and how this affects what people are demanding and why. It's not just about a good financial equation, it's about a good human equation.

Only through deep understanding and listening to what matters, and to what the problems are perceived to be on both sides, can the options that are *really* on the table be explored.

Shared knowledge

Leadership in pension management involves building the foundation for good decisions through shared knowledge.

Building good relationships with unions and their leaders can create pathways to pension best practices. That's because when it comes to putting new plans into action, "input that is gained from people, especially those that actually implement the plan... will become 'reality-based' and it minimizes the chance of leaving something out that is critical to an objective."[7] In other words, the why and how of the human part of the equation can be built in from the start.

Negotiations need to start with good information and deep knowledge of what will result in a positive financial or lifestyle-choice outcome for stakeholders. Good information starts with a commitment to shared knowledge management, well before the possibility of a barrier to a solid agreement between management and unions arises.

How can you make this work?

A useful starting point is to reflect on what is meant by data, information, knowledge, and the differences between these categories:

- **Data.** This means base statistics without any interpretation.
- **Information.** This is processed data—answers to who, what, where, and when questions.

- **Knowledge.** This is the application of data and information—answers to questions like "How can we get things done?"
- **Understanding.** This contains the answers to questions like "Why do we do this?"
- **Wisdom.** This is the application of knowledge and the evaluation of understanding.

Knowledge takes two forms:

- **Explicit knowledge.** This can be codified and communicated, and could be expressed as rules or guidelines or in other forms. This is the kind of knowledge that comes from, for example, information collected about how a pension is performing.
- **Tacit knowledge.** This is intangible, subjective, and not easily expressed, and people may not be aware of using it. This is the kind of knowledge that comes from, for example, the way in which people feel about a pension and its possibility for success as an incentive or tool.

Knowledge management asks us to look at an organization in terms of the relationships that cause knowledge to be created, shared, and, on the way, evaluated. From this perspective, businesses are viewed as needing to innovate and respond quickly in the face of the accelerating pace of change in a world of increasing complexity. This complexity comes as much from the speed and volume of information flow as from the increasingly global competitive environment. In this context, excellence comes from making the most of the knowledge held in an organization.

When it comes to pensions, sharing knowledge means the following:

- Business leaders need to share key drivers for a pension's financial success.
- Union leaders need to share key drivers for employee success.
- Both parties need to use this knowledge; they cannot ignore it.

Shared knowledge management starts with a cooperative style of management in which leaders are not the prime decision makers but rather first-stage moderators of processes and ideas. In this way, leaders contribute to effective knowledge creation, sharing, and evaluation by facilitating the environment and leading by personal example.

The typical union and corporate environments are often culturally and socially different from one where shared knowledge is the norm, as we can see in the table below.

Culture comparison

TYPICAL ORGANIZATIONAL CULTURE	KNOWLEDGE-SHARING CULTURE
imposed control	self-managed
appointed leaders	natural leaders
command and control	consultation
formal job descriptions	loosely defined jobs
vertical communications	lateral interaction
centralized	distributed
compartmentalized	crossing boundaries
independent	interdependent
inward looking	outward looking
passion for order	tolerance for ambiguity
conformity	valuing difference
personal knowledge	shared knowledge

Let's look at examples to help clarify how some of these factors work in real life, and how they apply to pension relations.

Air Canada

Air Canada used to have a defined benefits pension plan that they believed put them at a massive risk, and in 2003 they filed for bankruptcy protection on those grounds.[8] Their aim: to stop allowing new union hires to join their plan and thereby decrease their existing contributions. The union wasn't having it and, to find a solution that would serve both sides, years of negotiations ensued. It wasn't until 2011 that a new option was put on the table for a defined contribution plan, a hybrid defined benefit/defined contribution plan, *and* a multi-employer pension plan, each of which is available to employees.

The plan worked, and Air Canada's pensions went from deficit to surplus over the course of only four years. Essentially, the airline and the union agreed to move from imposed control to a self-managed, knowledge-sharing culture. Instead of their pension and their information being compartmentalized and ordered, they built a new pension strategy that crossed boundaries and created profitable ambiguity. There is flexibility, understanding, and idea sharing in this new plan, which has allowed for unprecedented success where there previously was failure.

Canada Post

A somewhat different set of outcomes took place at Canada Post when its defined benefit plan went into crisis. Without the buy-in of the union, the organization's leadership decided not to reinvest in the fund itself when the federal government offered money to offset losses.

Canada Post considered imposed control, with appointed leaders rather than a shared knowledge team of management and union representatives, to be the only way forward. With a solvency deficit of $184 million in 2003, Canada Post reported a $6.9 billion solvency deficit in 2015, based on the market value of these pension assets.[9] During this time, the organization had to continually boost the fund with solvency payments, and the federal government had to step in once again in 2014 to formally, albeit temporarily, manage the insolvency. Although there has been a new plan put into place, the level of collaboration between stakeholders remains an issue.

How can we shift towards a culture where shared knowledge management is likely to take place?

Knowledge sharing can only be volunteered, not compelled, so it needs to be easy. As we have seen throughout this chapter, research from the field shows that we learn a lot more from a story than a set of bare facts, as the act of telling triggers more reflection in the listener. Therefore, the first step to shifting the culture is to step away from abject negotiations towards listening and sharing.

To change the story, it is often useful to bring in *external, unbiased consultants or learning programs* that can help people discover their own sources of knowledge and understand the key drivers in pension management, especially because there are no easy answers. In this way, both unions and management teams can bring their own knowledge management leadership to bear and to bridge gaps between these groups.

Shifting expectations and standards with unions

Knowledge input from people, no matter what faction they favour or stakeholder group they belong to, leads to practical, reality-based solutions.

To this end, formulating a plan where unions and management teams work towards a pension plan together requires five key steps:[10]

- Facilitate teamwork from the start. Build shared learning processes, decision making, and rewards-orientation meetings in pension and rewards management. And invite all key stakeholders to contribute.
- Establish clear goals for each group in the company, and always remember where the company as a whole is already aligned.
- Empower the team on both sides to work towards new solutions that take the other stakeholders' values first.

- Create useful knowledge management processes, such as accessible policy banks, brainstorming scrums, and internal mentoring support systems, so that team idea generation and evaluation is possible, despite existing factional differences.
- Evaluate the ways in which ideas are generated as well as critical thinking skills through defined and agreed-upon metrics, so that better processes can be put into place for the future.

There are three key orientations that can move an organization towards these goals based on the recognition that businesses are human, social entities, and that human qualities can get in the way of practical solutions. These are broader, leadership-oriented (rather than pension-only) approaches that can alleviate standard barriers in management–union relations.

Needs orientation

First, an organization can take on a needs orientation. The company can review its employees' stated or unstated pension needs so that it can build a performance management system that is more sustainable over the long term—one that is not based on financial costs alone and connects back to the needs of all of its stakeholders.

Using this approach, an organization has to move away from its perception of the value of pension investment as related to costs alone. The firm will have to shift the way that it rewards leadership and mentoring, and create a new focus on union success that looks at how needs in the firm can be supported so that capacity increases. This approach can lead to a high level of alignment between the needs of stakeholders and the outcomes of the firm. The major disadvantage of it, however, is that this approach may require a significant cultural change in a union environment and, if it does, will take more time to implement than the company may be willing to spend, given how the costs of human resources are currently perceived in typical union-based organizations.

Resource orientation

Second, an organization can take on a resource orientation. This means that a company can change its performance and pension management system to one that matches resources both within the firm and externally. Consider the kind of financial and human resources that the company has and compare them with what they want to have. What's the gap? Does the organization have a high level of attrition, for example, and is this affecting revenues? Drilling down to this level can help the company create strategies that ensure that costs align with spending on pensions. In this way, performance management can become a resource in and of itself.

This approach requires a change in values, with the company seeing its human resources as something that ought not to be overtaxed because, in the long term, doing so would likely lead to a decrease in knowledge resources, which would, in turn, negatively affect sales and revenues. Through methods specific to their company, human resource leaders can support a resource orientation so that shared psychosocial and work experiences are seen as a resource that can be tapped to increase revenues, emphasizing how unions provide value to an organization.[11] The advantage of this approach is that stakeholder investors may be amenable to the positioning of employees as a resource that needs to be maintained, lest it be lost. The major disadvantage is that this approach may still result in the perception of unions as cost centres to be controlled.

Process orientation

Third, an organization can take on a process orientation. An organization can change its retirement management system to build in metrics that reward union members based on how they engage in the process of building and delivering on goals.

This approach is grounded in a performance engagement strategy that relies on 360-degree or multi-rater feedback to allow the organization to assess its union employees' needs with competency models, and to identify key people to fill critical functions related to supporting work processes and staff. This approach will lead to a high level of internal capacity that can connect metrics with process aims so that negotiations may become easier, whether the discussion is about pensions or any other employee wage or benefit scheme. The major disadvantage is that this approach can lead to confusion about the roles of individuals in each working group, and may increase the costs of pension management and negotiation with union leaders.

Change must happen

No matter what approach is taken, connecting with unions and their leaders can create pathways to pension best practices, but the reality is that the divide between management and unions must shift and, ultimately, decrease in order to build organizational capacity. We can see this in the Air Canada example: when push came to shove and all stakeholders had their say, not only could a hybrid solution be created, but this approach also resulted in better pension outcomes for all parties.

Union–management relationships can be very entrenched, but we in the pension business know that the need to look at more flexible pension plans that work for people's lives is forcing change. So are retirement plans in a world where our social expectations and labour demographics are shifting quickly. Both parties will benefit from opening up to a knowledge-sharing culture, but, perhaps even more important, there may be no choice in the matter. Pensions, and people, need to be more flexible and reflexive if they are going to be sustained.

8

PENSIONS AND THE FUTURE OF WORK

PENSION BENEFITS ARE critically important for workers deciding whether to accept a job or stay with their current employer, according to recent global research. In fact, 68 per cent of workers in a 2018, ten-country study by Accenture stated that pension benefits were a critical factor, and 84 per cent of respondents reported that they wanted to use company-based retirement planning services.[1] Younger workers will switch jobs with increasing frequency to get what they want, resulting in lost talent investments. At the same time, increasingly, people will work past age sixty-five to secure adequate resources for retirement, in part because they haven't planned ahead or aren't earning enough to save.[2] Another factor is that government-provided flat-rate pensions and unemployment benefits are well below subsistence needs for a single adult in most countries around the world, including Canada and the UK.[3]

For companies to attract the right talent and keep it for the right length of time, pension decision-making processes need to adapt to what pundits believe the workforce will expect in the future. The challenge is that the future may not take the form that we expect, and adaptation to the future of work is likely a necessary shift for most companies.

We need to discuss what future employees will want from their pensions and how we can create better targets for pensions based on expectations about the future of work. And we need to understand the responsibilities in pension management, not just in the sense of compliance but also in terms of impact on the future, people's lives, and economic development. In this chapter, we'll discuss what we might be able to do to develop healthy, well-performing pensions that have an ethical and long-term purpose in mind, and how to create a clear framework for making pension decisions.

Digging deeper into the true challenges of creating a future-proof pension plan, and not just taking the easy path in the short term, is most important.

The future of work and pensions

Organizations of the future need to position themselves strategically in competitive labour markets by responding to an inelastic supply and, therefore, a high level of demand for key employees.

This is especially true in a globalized labour market where workers can transcend borders to deliver specialized skills and experience.[4] With some jobs being outsourced to the developing world because of advances in telecom and Internet technologies that ease the burden of distributed labour engagement, the need for employees with definitive skills is on the rise. So, workers are becoming choosier, especially when they know that there are better options around every corner. In other words, companies need to increase their ability to connect with new employees through broad job advertising and social network development, but they also have to appeal to workers through the delivery of employment support such as better salaries, transportation or relocation bonuses, flexible work arrangements, and pensions.[5]

Nonetheless, with respect to talent management, although CEOs and senior executives are purported to perceive people as paramount, they have not necessarily backed this ideal in practical terms. According to a 2017 article, although people are seen as a company's "most important asset... [CEOs] have not behaved accordingly when it comes to developing their business strategies, their organization designs, and their talent management practices."[6] This means there is a lack of alignment between what leaders believe ought to be done to support their teams, which is based on old-fashioned carrot-and-stick management, and what human resource managers know will work, which is providing stability, care, and good pensions for employees. It is heartening to know that CEOs and human resource managers share a belief in the relative importance of people; however, the differences between the perceptions of executives and human resource managers are significant, and the reality is that executives' decisions matter most when it comes to pensions.

How we can create better targets and objectives for pensions based on expectations about the future of work?

A recent article from *Forbes* reports that members of the Business Roundtable, an association of more than 180 chief executive officers of America's leading companies, have signed a statement prioritizing people over profits.[7] One of the tenets of this statement is to offer *real* retirement plans, namely, those that account for true human needs after years of service to companies.

Understanding that individuals need to be psychologically engaged to ensure that they are committed and motivated to achieve on the job is important. Members of the Business Roundtable recognize that attention paid to the psychosocial environment of a workplace increases the likelihood that the company will reach its goals.

Pensions, in a psychologically safe company, become a means by which to stimulate organizational change.

This can shift organizational culture over the short and the long term, encourage employers and employees to remain committed, and so build the company from the inside out. Individuals need to receive support so that the firm can retain their knowledge and continue to build collaborative networks that share resources. Companies must keep their employees fulfilled both extrinsically and intrinsically. In short, for peak performance to continue, employees have to feel as if they are part of a family and that their contributions are valued.[8]

Some companies prefer to offer performance-based bonuses as a means to incentivize employees, rather than pensions, which they would receive no matter what outcomes they achieve. In other words, company leaders believe that profit incentives motivate people better than pensions do.

The popular profit-based incentive plans are flawed, as we've discussed previously. In most situations companies would be better off creating pension plans.

A pragmatic application of pension management is to create an environment in which employees are encouraged and facilitated to feel safe and secure. This results in more focused employees and can, over time, result in an adaptive, productive, and innovative organization.

Responsibilities in pension management

What is our responsibility in pension management? The simple answer is that *we need to give people faith in the future.*

More than anything, that's what people are looking for from their organization's leaders. They want to know, at the end of the day, that there's a better future ahead, and that you have their best interests in mind. The responsibility in pension management—not just in the sense of compliance but in terms of impact on the future, people's lives, and economic development—is to provide a means for employees to focus on their jobs rather than on how they will pay their mortgage, on their level of stress, or on a requirement to achieve something beyond their job description.

Performance is important to employees, but perhaps not as important a motivator as companies perceive. That's why compensation policies, including pensions, need to connect all team members together in their work experience, and to this end, financial rewards should be tied to employees' commitment to the company, rather than to their day-to-day progress.[9] To meet the needs of future workers, the objectives of an effective pension program are to create support systems that integrate not only financial reward but also employee motivation tactics linked to security, rather than to performance alone. According to statistics that have been tracked over the last thirty years by researchers at the State University of New York at Buffalo and the University of Wisconsin–Madison, pension strategy is part of a culture that values "achievement, recognition, work itself, responsibility, advancement, and professional growth, [and there is a] positive correlation between job satisfaction and an employees' mental well-being, commitment to the job, and motivational factors."[10] This creates the foundation for internal alignment and a means for employees to feel rewarded in their job on a psychological level, something that is underlined for them when they have access to a well-designed pension.

To develop healthy, well-performing pensions that have an ethical and long-term purpose in mind, therefore, it is necessary to look at pension planning from a holistic perspective rather than based on the interests and needs of a small group of stakeholders at the top of the organization.

A stressed workforce, in which people feel that they have to compete for money or where their pension compensation is at risk in economically unstable times, is not good for the long-term growth of a business. Instead, pension rewards that make employees feel recognized for their skills and commitment are a good way of providing rewards for positive activity in the organization. This is a tried and tested way of building capacity and collaboration.

Pension decisions for the future of work

Leaders of organizations thinking about pensions for a future talent landscape need to manage things differently.

As noted in a report on the future of jobs from the World Economic Forum, no longer is talent a long-term issue that can be solved with successful approaches used in the past.[11] Instead, proactive, reactive, and innovative pension management is an urgent issue. The following tenets need to be addressed in order for pensions to be aligned with the future of work.

Adaptive human resources strategies

Human resource management needs to become more strategic, and, therefore, when it comes to pensions, the HR team has to have a seat at the table. They can provide insights to help organizations align their business, talent, and pension management strategies to maximize available opportunities and adapt to transformational trends in our shifting workforces around the globe.

Communication and pension training

The future of work, notes the World Economic Forum, is marked by a need for increased training in the use of all benefits, including pensions, at all levels. Training is a missing link that affects a range of industries, not just blue-collar jobs: people do not understand how their benefits work and even why they have them in the first place. One common flaw in plan delivery is that plan sponsors fail to clearly explain to their employees the purpose, objectives, and rules of the plan and employees' responsibility to optimize their benefits. Setting up a plan and delegating its administration to a service provider or consultant is not enough. The plan sponsor should make sure employees know about the tools available to help them plan their finances and meet their retirement goals. By contrast, gaining an understanding of how employees perceive the value proposition of pension and benefit plans can give directors invaluable information for use when creating or changing the structure of employee compensation, and of pensions and benefits in particular. Seeking input from employees, internally or from the market, can help the organization win buy-in for changes and identify potential hurdles to implementation.[12] Leaders need to explore optimal training programs for employees at all levels of the organization and work with HR to make sure that these are effective.

Portable pensions

Given the complexity of the working world, the future of work will be marked by more rapid changes in talent as people move on to different companies. According to the World Economic Forum report we've been discussing in this chapter, businesses will need to collaborate on talent issues, rather than compete, in order to be strategic, and this includes providing portable benefits packages. Businesses should work with industry partners to pool resources and maximize benefits, and work more closely with governments to identify where there will be options to increase and match RSP contributions, for example. The future of work is also flexible. Leveraging flexible working arrangements and online talent platforms means that physical and organizational boundaries are blurring, and organizations are going to have to become significantly more agile in their thinking about managing people's work and the workforce as a whole. For pensions, this means that many programs will need to cross geographical boundaries and become agile to meet the needs of different working communities and cultures.

Data analytics

Organizations will need to build a new approach to pension planning and talent management, where they will increasingly rely on both internal and external data to understand best practices, and to plan for their own futures. Organizations will need to seek out data sources that match their needs, with the assistance of a pension management consultant or their accountants, and create metrics that work over the long term.

Ethics, privacy, and transparency

Talent diversity means pension diversity. The World Economic Forum shows that gender, age, ethnicity, and sexual orientation are well-known barriers to benefit equity in developed countries around the world, and this needs to be addressed, all the while keeping privacy intact. In addition, as diversity issues are addressed in the workplace, investment issues related to pension choice are also being brought to light. Environmental, social, and governance (ESG) factors, according to the Financial Services Commission of Ontario (FSCO), ought to be considered when it comes to pension planning. This means that pension managers ought to vet how a company or industry in which they invest interacts with the physical environment, how it impacts a community or society, and how the countries in which their investments are located are governed.

All of these issues will become more and more important to future workforces, and, therefore, a company ought to determine the underlying ethical boundaries of its pension practices.

The future is now

We know that pensions matter to people, but the realities of our workforce and our organizations are changing more quickly than ever before. That's why the future of work requires us to think ahead and make strategic plans now, so that we can ensure that the right people are on board to help us create exceptional, growing businesses.

Creating a future-proof pension plan is possible. What future employees will want is the ability to collaborate with their organizational leaders to choose the right pension package for themselves, and to port that pension if and when they leave. This means that new responsibilities in pension management need to account for ethical and long-term goals, rather than short-term internal wins.

To develop healthy, well-performing pensions that have a future purpose in mind, organizations need to partner with their employees to explore what matters to them, delve into their data, and deliver a talent-friendly solution.

9

THE FUTURE TECH OF PENSIONS

CAN PENSION PLANS survive and even thrive in an environment of rapid change while at the same time meet the rising demand for cost-effective old-age finance?

FinTech players, namely, those companies that create technological solutions for the financial services industry, have transformed the financial services space in the last five years. These players have brought extensive reach, agility, innovation, and low-cost operating models to address the varied problems and pain points of the industry, all the while driving up efficiencies.

Can pensions benefit from accelerated collaborations with FinTech players? It may be possible to develop innovative solutions that improve awareness and increase reach for pension products. As pension plan managers and organizational leaders know, technology has long been an important part of the delivery of financial solutions;

FinTech is different because its efforts allow software to play a larger and more comprehensive role than in the past. It can broaden what we use data for, how we integrate it into decision making, and how we individualize investment opportunities at a granular level, driven by a belief that technology can create pathways to success that can't be operationalized in any other way.

Should leaders in pension management consider these new and, in some cases, untested pathways? In this chapter, we'll talk about the high-tech scope of future retirement options, the possibility of increasing flexibility for pension funds through more avenues of investment targeting younger workforces, and the use of end-to-end digital processes to decrease costs for the future of pensions. We'll also discuss the risks of FinTech as it currently stands.

Can we leverage this technology for the betterment of all of our pensions, both for organizations and for investors? Let's find out.

A new alliance

Pension funds, as major, long-term investment management tools, are going to be an important part of the FinTech transformation of money exchanges that we expect to take place over the next few decades.[1]

In essence, FinTech connects to how individual and group investment accounts are created. That much everyone knows: most, if not all, pension clients can now log in to systems that show them where their money is, how it is growing, and how they can change beneficiaries, mutual funds, and other options.

But FinTech companies are aiming to increase the ability of pension managers to securely segregate members' accounts to allow them to be individually customized. By linking these accounts to financial markets and payment options, pension plans will be both transparent and flexible. Pension holders will be able to not only see what they have invested but also make choices more concretely. They will be able to look at their own data, such as their current pension value, and compare it with other options available to them. In addition, any potential trade-offs between taking money out now and leaving it for a longer period of time could be more visible.

This won't make forecasting fund performance any easier than it is at present. But FinTech will make it possible for companies and individuals to be better informed about the possible effects of their choices, at the click of a button. It will allow for better tracking of actuarial data for companies' pension managers, and it will allow for big data integration so that individual organizations can assess where they are in pension value and viability in comparison to others in their industry. Finally, FinTech will create a more streamlined means by which back and mid-office pension services teams can work with all this data to make better decisions going forward.

FinTech players have already developed considerable expertise in the areas of credit and payments, which could be leveraged and channelled into retirement savings.

The high-tech scope of future retirement options

In Peru, FinTech strategies have created a whole new level of opportunity for private pension funds that has the potential to change the game for us all, worldwide.

In the opinion of Jorge Mogrovejo, who is the deputy superintendent of private pension funds supervision for the Superintendency of Banking, Insurance, and Pension Funds Administrators of Peru, strategies to increase retirement savings are a major priority.[2] He explained to his audience at the International Organisation of Pension Supervisors (IOPS) conference for the OECD that millennials in his country are lagging behind their elders when it comes to saving for the future, and he is working hard to prevent long-term poverty.

But instead of instituting forced pension investments, which are on the table for some countries, such as those in the UK, Mogrovejo is taking an inventive, private pension model that has all of the hallmarks of long-term success. In essence, he has created a program in which building retirement savings could be based on consumer buying habits rather than income, amalgamating the consumption habits of millennials with new digital pension offerings. Through a driving partnership model with various financial institutions, leading corporations, and public organizations, Mogrovejo has allowed private pension plan administrators to partner with commercial institutions such as retail businesses, pharmacies, and supermarkets. Each of these institutions offers discounts on purchases of goods and services, and a portion of every transaction is credited to their customers' pension account. If that account is managed through their employer, it is topped up through matching funds. No matter what the origin of the funds, however, the country has invested in the pension infrastructure with its FinTech partners to make the plan available to all citizens and, in turn, to top up funds for poorer community members and provide instant tax benefits.

The results are outstanding. Individuals win because they are forced to save, and saving is made easy. Organizations win because the process drives business growth and builds simplicity into pension planning at work. Governments win because there is less potential for negative socio-economic trends for retirees, which will cost less in taxation spending. According to the World Bank, this approach has spurred a renewal of pension investing in Peru as well as the widespread opening of bank accounts created specifically for collecting pension monies, accounting for almost one million new pension plan investors in that country.[3]

The Peru initiative is only the tip of the iceberg. Currently, FinTech options in the private sector allow for low-cost alternatives for small- and medium-sized businesses, for example. Web platforms and mobile applications can also allow pension investors to instantly top up their monthly funds, which encourages participants, especially younger workers, to start planning for their future.[4]

Increasing flexibility for pension funds

FinTech makes it possible to increase flexibility for pension funds through more avenues of investment that target younger workforces.

In a recent study in Europe presented at the International Organization of Securities Commissions (IOSCO) conference, it was found that pension fund management would, over the long term, benefit from a behavioural approach to both fund creation and individualization, based on pension investors' personalities.[5] Personality has an immense impact on the way people participate in pensions, beyond what we may have assumed in the past, and this ought to be taken into consideration when we plan pension rollouts and internal learning schemes. As noted in the findings from this study, which matched indicators from a Myers-Briggs personality test with pension behaviours, financial personality has implications for financial behaviour. Extroverts are willing and ready to talk to financial advisors but introverts prefer written material. Sensory people like to deal with facts, but thinking-preference people manage their money in a rational, impersonal way. People with feeling preferences may be interested in socially responsible investments, but those with perceiving preferences do not like to plan in advance.

When we look at all these different personality types and how they make financial decisions, it is clear how and why pension managers struggle to ensure that everyone in their company understands their pension, its impact, and their choices. This is something that, as we have discussed in past chapters, has emerged as a leading concern for organizations in Canada, no matter what plan structure is in place. Because individuals have emotional, rather than purely factual and rational, ties to their money and their future planning, we cannot ignore the importance of these kinds of findings.

In turn, these findings are linked to FinTech because, as noted in the IOSCO conference report, FinTech can use operational and survey data to create a user engagement plan that is flexible to individuals' needs and their investment preferences. This approach is not a be-all and end-all structure but rather is a way for pension managers to hone their employee offerings and allow for better individual outcomes on, say, defined contribution plans. It will decrease the risk for investors and increase their ability to work towards certain outcomes. These kinds of options are only available, note the IOSCO conference leaders, when the big data used by FinTech is integrated into individual pension plans. By using big data and providing their employees with digital assessments of their choices and preferred behaviours, organizational leaders may create more balance, commitment, and comfort for their teams.

At present, only a few leading companies, like Microsoft, are delving into pension management products in this space, with their intelligent banking platform, integrating artificial intelligence, blockchain, and investment strategies. Even these ideas, however, are just being explored in research and have yet to roll out in any substantive way.[6] But as we see these offerings expanded and increased, they may become more readily available to all pension managers and business leaders.

End-to-end digital processes

The use of end-to-end digital processes can decrease costs for the future of pensions. FinTech can lower transaction costs and enable new financial alternatives for those participating in pensions. It can also increase compliance throughout pension management and in individual employee engagement, allowing for better tracking of systems, participation, and risks. We likely already understand these financial technological tools because they have become part of our day-to-day understanding of banking transactions in the modern world.

On top of these benefits, FinTech can also improve information-sharing processes and financial decision making.[7] When large-scale databases were first being developed, the focus of their creation for business protocols was the management of customer relationships. The purpose of this effort was to organize customers demographically into microsegments and later into psychographic groups, so that users could target marketing to each of these groups and, as a result, increase revenues and decrease costs; efforts were no longer wasted in appealing to certain demographic and psychographic sectors of business engagement. When it comes to pensions, this can happen in more depth with FinTech data. Meeting the needs of a set of employee investors, or any other group, requires the automation of processes. In using the amalgamated data from each step in these processes, public and private organizations can create demand for pension services, which can also include ease of use, streamlined interactions, and more customer loyalty. Information including internal and external data, and consumer, supplier, and competitor data can be merged to increase revenue or decrease costs.

As a whole, this means that FinTech presents

- a unified database and set of pension-oriented algorithms;
- a system that can store and synchronize real-time information from individuals, suppliers, organizational leaders, and government entities;
- the opportunity to help organizations build efficiencies and increase the delivery and reach of pension services;
- the support necessary to ensure that everyone can engage easily with external stakeholders like investment platforms;
- the ability to increase compliance to the regulations of industries; and
- a more flexible and focused means to create the foundation for long-term growth.

Think about it. We may not be doing all this data management at the present time, but we will be able to use these tools in the future, to plan differently and hopefully in a way that will better benefit all stakeholders, because more information can lead to better decisions.

The risks

We are only just beginning to explore the ways in which FinTech can impact our pension futures, according to field research and practical tests. What is happening in Peru, for example, is a concerted effort and investment process on the part of a federal government, which means that it is not necessarily going to be available in Canada anytime soon. As well, many of the tools discussed in this chapter are only just beginning to be developed for the pension market.

So, what risks are we facing at present?

FinTech's big data itself may not be valuable for a few more years. For example, the privacy issues around data mining processes for pensions are still being addressed. Financial initiatives, especially those linked to government regulations and data, are likely to include the strictest level of protocols for data protection. As well, whichever data solution an organization chooses for merging data from its disparate entities, there are going to be gaps. This is because of shifts in the ways that data is used and challenges in technological solutions adapting themselves to multiple forms of data.

In addition, to use data effectively for pension management, we need a computational framework that allows for the collection, visualization, retention, ability to obtain, and repackaging of data in different ways. We must consider pension design, service delivery, and external stakeholder engagement as we begin imagining how data can be used. We must also ensure that the organization is prepared to effectively manage this data in concert with stakeholders, and what this will physically look like. For a pension data-mining project to work well, for example, individual client or population needs, internal organizational capabilities, and the strategic goals of the organization all need to be considered during the project's development, well before it is put into action.

Although, as noted by the Canadian Public Pension Leadership Council, FinTech companies are backed by significant venture financing, and are challenging traditional models of financial services in banking, insurance, and wealth and investment management, these implementation risks have to be managed if pensions will successfully integrate their processes with this large-scale data.[8]

Forging ahead

We need to pay attention to FinTech. As the Canadian Public Pension Leadership Council suggests, integrating FinTech into pension management is a foregone conclusion, but prudence is still necessary. Even though, as the council stated, "exploration is already underway about how blockchain or some other form of distributed ledger technology could be used to improve transparency, efficiency, and trust in pensions,"[9] we are still years away from the capacity to achieve these goals. We're still not sure how the FinTech industry and these dynamics of the global economy are going to affect pension planning in the next few years.

With FinTech, the core value proposition that pensions offer people—the ability to meet their retirement income needs efficiently—can be maintained more readily than ever before. But we can't move in that direction without a great deal more research, testing, and confidence in these tools.

Despite the need for clarity on some of these issues, we're hopeful that this kind of technology will eventually present a new level of opportunity for pension managers across Canada, even as soon as in 2025. These technological solutions may provide us with deeper data, better engagement, and more successful plans for companies and pension investors alike. We've already been observing how some FinTech tactics have made present-day pension management less expensive and easier to implement. In the future, end-to-end digital processes will likely drive up pension growth opportunities, and do so in a way that is increasingly easy for all stakeholders.

It's not a great leap to imagine just how successful pension management might be in the future if we can move confidently, and carefully, towards a tech-informed pension environment.

10

HOW TO SUPPORT PENSION TRUSTEES AND YOUR ORGANIZATION

WHEN ASKED WHAT makes it difficult for them to plan for the future of their businesses, pension trustees regularly cite issues such as lack of time, resources, knowledge, and information.[1] The more complex our global economic system becomes, the more that level of stress increases.

It's all too common for pension trustees to worry that they're not doing their jobs. And the challenge is that they may be correct. Pension trustees may be directly failing at building and protecting pensions, and we may not even know it.

Research conducted in the UK in 2019, as we'll discuss further below, shows that most boards of trustees rate their own effectiveness highly, and perhaps much more highly than they should, given that they rarely internally review that effectiveness with accurate metrics.[2] In fact, as the International Centre for Pension Management at the University of Toronto's Rotman School of Business claims, there isn't even evidence to show that *independent* reviews of boards of trustees are effective.[3] In other words, boards worry about their collective ability to make informed and timely decisions about their pension responsibilities and implement them effectively but don't often dig deep enough to figure out what's going wrong.

But what about trustees' work in the first place? Do we need to be *that* concerned?

Apparently, we do. Even if pension trustees receive training and, through their role, accumulate experience in financial markets, field research shows that they make decisions, by and large, for reasons that are not financial.[4] Who they know, what their biases are, and what they've read in the news that week may factor more significantly into pension trustees' decisions than serving the pension's strategic intent.

So, what's going on? What happens when good governance relies on people who aren't fully prepared and supported?

We need to delve into key issues around building an outstanding board of trustees for your pension goals, such as finding and appointing suitable people from both the member-nominated and the company-nominated options. In this chapter, we'll talk about how to develop a clear agenda, terms of reference, critical delegations, good advice, and a robust audit trail. Finally, we'll examine how to facilitate assessments to highlight shortcomings even where trustee confidence is high.

Building an outstanding board of trustees

Before we explore best practices, we have to understand what's already going wrong on boards of trustees.

The biggest challenge to pensions is that boards are closed social networks in which decisions are absent from public checks and balances.[5] Boards easily become echo chambers marked by low-stakes decision making rather than strategic aims.

Despite that there are increasing regulations to challenge these closed networks, the pool of trustees continues to be very small, with senior executives sometimes sitting on many different boards at the same time. Decisions made by one company can begin to echo those made by others, even in the same field, which further deepens social ties and embeds poor practices across firms. The core challenge is, then, that boards are not created in the best interest of a company or its stakeholders.

Recent research has shown that opening up the social network and adding gender, racial, ethnic, and other forms of diversity to boards can increase financial success for a company, over the short and the long term. And yet 40 per cent of public companies—whether corporate, pension, or non-profit—do not include women on their boards. Including women and people of colour results in better attendance to government regulations and financial accounting structures as well, leading to fewer ethical compliance issues. Yet this inclusion is simply not happening.[6]

A recent study in Canada, for example, found that many business leaders wrongly assume that women are not as committed to business development as men are, or do not have the skills for board management, and so are not offered board positions as often.[7] The reverse has been proved true, in that corporate and pension boards are likely to financially benefit from the appointment of women directors—boards with women equal better decisions and an increase in financial success. Even so, the contribution of women directors on boards can often depend on their ability to make alliances with influential board members, which may not be possible because of closed social networks. In other words, the reason for women's exclusion from boards is not based on their efficacy or their ability to engage investors, but rather on false assumptions about their worth and ability to contribute. Not prioritizing women's participation, as well as the participation of a range of diverse individuals, ultimately, can limit a board's potential to serve its stakeholders.

What does all of this mean?

The onus is on organizations to choose *good pension trustees*. Instead of simply choosing the closest or most familiar individuals for the task, organizational leaders must *strategically and methodologically* select pension trustees.

Given this high bar, how can you find pension trustees who meet these criteria?

A Canadian study on recruiting pension trustees found that the most effective method to is to use a human resource management approach in which the position is listed, and candidates are interviewed based on their experience and skills and are vetted by third parties.[8] The job description should be thorough and explicit. Nominations should be eschewed. Candidates should be able to apply from within the company and without, but using an independent human resource or pension management consulting firm could help ensure that the process is unbiased. Once candidates with the appropriate competencies have been found, they ought to be onboarded, trained, and engaged in the same way as others in the firm.

What makes a good pension trustee?

An extended study that was initiated by the Working Group of the Trustee Leadership Forum for Retirement Security, a project of the Initiative for Responsible Investment at the Harvard Kennedy School, stated that there are seven key traits that make trustees good at their job.[9]

In your pension trustee search, you should recruit people with these traits:

- **The strength not to be intimidated.** Pension trustees must have a fundamental sense of strength and self-awareness so that they can make decisions on their own. This is the core skill, the Kennedy School suggests, that underlines the rest of the skills to follow.
- **The willingness to be perpetually inquisitive.** Pension trustees have to be interested in their pension work. They aren't simply following the tide; they have the wherewithal to discover what's new and different in the pension industry, and be critical of what they find, so that they can provide the best advice for their team.
- **The strength to be unwaveringly ethical.** This goes without saying, but pension trustees should be chosen from among those who are the most trustworthy and have experience keeping to an ethical framework. An up-and-coming executive or a go-getter may not have the right state of mind to protect the assets of a whole workforce and consider all stakeholder needs.
- **The ability and willingness to articulate clear, unbiased thinking.** This is a tough one. In the study cited above, individuals nominated by the members of the pension fund

and those put forward by the company are often much more likely to base decisions on the recommendations of others, rather than doing their own research. Decisions are too fast and too biased to make the right impact, and are mired by confirmation bias. Pension trustees ought to be independent thinkers who won't vote via groupthink.

- **The strength and willingness to be diligent.** Let alone doing their own external research, pension trustees have to be willing to at least read and digest the materials that are put in front of them. If they aren't inclined or, more frequently a problem, don't have the time, then pension management is not for them.
- **The ability to not be blinded by the deliberate distractors.** Trustees are perpetually faced with distractions. The Kennedy School suggests that a lot of factions in pension decisions lobby pension trustees to follow their lead. These should not influence the decision-making process at all.
- **The ability to be great listeners and interlocutors.** Pension trustees look for ways to bring people together without advancing a single opinion, instead building on stakeholder ideas and knowledge to create a great plan.

Developing a clear agenda

Pension trustees set an agenda that has its own set of values and responsibilities and must reflect the firm's overarching business strategy. These matters are typically detailed in the organization's bylaws. The bylaws commonly also specify the number of members of the board, how they are to be chosen, and when they are to meet, but there needs to be a strategy in place that provides incentive to debate what really matters to stakeholders and how to reach goals effectively. This process is about alignment: a pension plan has to reflect organizational strategy so that everyone is working towards the same outcomes.

Canadian research shows that the average agenda of pension trustees needs to significantly evolve.[10] Apart from the pension itself, several practices for the agenda must be put into place for trustees to work effectively:

- **Develop a self-improvement culture on the board.** The board of trustees has to want to work towards best practices, so that it can develop and maintain general standards aimed at improving the governance practices of pension funds. The culture of the board should reflect the needs of the organization and the traits for good governance noted above.
- **Create a defined strategy.** A board's activities are determined by the powers, duties, and responsibilities delegated

to it or conferred on it by an authority outside itself. Nonetheless, pension trustees ought to draft a scheme business plan that includes the pension scheme's objectives, long-terms goals, and how they propose to meet them.

- **Provide a deep understanding of the board's mission and its investment beliefs.** This is where alignment comes in. Business and pension need to go hand in hand. Structures that better align interests of service providers with those of fund participants and beneficiaries will serve all stakeholders more completely. Every year, this mission statement should be revisited and affirmed, or changed to reflect new focus areas.

- **Create a code of ethics.** The trustees need to have their own ethical code that begins with regulatory norms but goes beyond them. This can be achieved by placing the impetus on best practices in governance in ethical terms. Without an underlying standard for ethics, which is kept in check by a strong board, company or collective agreement leaders may aim for more than they can handle.

- **Ensure lower risks for trustee decision.** Evidence of excessive investment herding, where people just follow the patterns of investment that they already know rather than subject these patterns to critical thinking, is frequent in Canadian pension plans—including by all participants and beneficiaries. A risk management strategy that creates checks and balances for trustee actions can help alleviate this.

- **Create clarity in all responsibilities.** Make sure that pension trustees' agenda items are based on their job descriptions and nothing else: overstepping the bounds of these responsibilities can lead to conflicts between the board and other stakeholders. Consideration should be given to a "comply or explain" reporting approach on compliance with best practices to provide flexibility.
- **Create clarity in record keeping.** Pension trustees should have specific frameworks for decision making, governance structures, and processes. These should be documented clearly at every meeting.
- **Mandate regular external trustee audits.** This is not a financial audit, but an external test of possible conflicts of interest and compliance to the business strategy. All trustees ought to be subject to dismissal and/or prosecution if they break the letter or the underlying values of this code of ethics.

Facilitating trustee assessments

As we've discussed above, currently boards are a closed social network in which decisions are absent from public opinion or interest and, therefore, there is a significant need for their work to be overseen, despite their independence. Even with diversity processes in place, pension boards of trustees can still become echo chambers in which the thoughts and desires of those in power are replicated. When this takes place, the board can't easily execute its key role: the critical assessment of pension activities.

Decisions also need to be subject to ample criticism in order for a company to move forward on new pension initiatives, and the diversity of opinion that is likely to occur in a more informed and professional board will serve this purpose. Even so, a company is working in its stakeholders' best interests if it can regularly and fully engage in a board review process so that stakeholders can protect their interests, ideas, and values, as well as their bottom lines, over the long term through positive board tactics.[11]

Pension trustees should already have their pension strategy and business plan and associated key metrics in place so that they can be assessed on an ongoing basis, as with any other business plan. But facilitating trustee assessments must go deeper than financial checks and balances.

There are three ways that assessments can take place:

- **Review.** Start by interviewing trustees on a regular basis or using an individual performance review of board members, similar to other human resource processes, to open up communication and address issues as soon as they come up. This is not a call for micromanagement but rather a means to build effective working relationships between the board and the pension management team. Understanding and addressing challenges at the individual trustee level will drive improvement in overall board effectiveness.

- **Reflect.** Create a reflection-based culture and ask for regular feedback about specific pension challenges and proposals through trustee surveys at board meetings. These can be quick processes meant to get a snapshot of ideas trustees have for the future, predictive risk issues, or other potential changes in the pension environment that will affect the business and its pension stakeholders. Steer away from in-depth discussion when it isn't necessary, to keep focus and ensure that powerful individuals do not overly sway outcomes.
- **Report.** When we don't adequately specify the methods of evaluating pension performance right from the beginning, we don't capture important pension performance data that could impact the timely discovery of problems. It could also mislead the pension management team about other project goals that were not specifically detailed. Key performance metrics have to be defined and checked, and there needs to be an iterative process for updating and improving outcomes based on those metrics.

But let's also be clear: employing performance metrics for pension planning shouldn't be based only on meeting financial goals, but also on 360-degree or multiple-constituency feedback that takes place as often as it is needed.

As we've mentioned, critical challenges in pension trustee work have been tied to groupthink and political power plays, and this leads to less effective outcomes for pensions, no matter how tight the purse strings. Leaning in to a feedback-based culture will allow not only multiple stakeholders to feel as if they are being heard and, therefore, more empowered to positively change, but also the organization to assess its pension trustee needs with competency models. It is possible, and even likely, that your organization will choose to remove pension trustees from their positions when they don't prove effective.

Let's do it right the first time

Having the right structure, the right processes, and the right people involved in running a pension scheme makes sense, but we must proceed with a business orientation. Trustees must be provided with the right skills to not only mitigate the risks a pension plan will face over the long term but also capitalize on any short-term market opportunities.

How can pension trustees step back from the processes, procedures, tools, and issues that surround their board daily and consider, "Could we be working more effectively?" or "How could we do things better?"

It all starts with a pension trustee culture that is professional, purposeful, and practical. Creating a board with people who know your business is not enough: they also have to want to know the pension business, and they have to be people who can be trusted with decisions upon which families and business leaders alike can depend.

You can align pension trustees with your business and the organization's purpose and goals. It's not just what you want for your pensions, but also what you want for your businesses, organizations, customers, and employees that matters. You can tap into insights about how your way of managing pensions—from communication to risk management strategies—can help you to achieve your desired organizational outcomes and impact.

Let's demand business sense from our pension trustees, and ask for a long-term performance orientation that moves everyone forward.

11

PARITY DISPARITY, THE PENSION ISSUE OF THE FUTURE

IT CAN BE argued that there are at least two fundamental goals of retirement savings. First, pensions are aimed at guaranteeing a basic level of retirement income for all employees. Second, pensions are meant to assist pension members in avoiding a serious disruption of their pre-retirement standard of living upon retirement.

But what if all pensions are not alike? What if the ability of employees across our society to benefit from pensions differs in ways that we cannot readily observe? What if what's going on underneath the surface is more important than the numbers on our retirement savings statements?

The idea of *pension parity* is that pensions have to be not only valuable but also fair and equitable, and, at the same time, they have to decrease members' risk exposure. This is difficult to achieve, especially because there are so many facets of understanding and operationalizing parity when it comes to pensions.

Achieving parity means that pensions have to be adequately funded, and risk-averse, which is the opposite of what most corporate pensions are planning for at the present.[1] In addition, pensions, at their core, are created to provide a future in retirement for members, but that isn't always the reality members face. Not only are there differences in how much money a person can expect to earn on their pension because of issues based on age, gender, and other social differences, but there are also fundamental challenges in the type of pensions that are chosen and operationalized. Over time, this can affect retirement, security, and health for all Canadians. When similar pension contribution rates result in vastly different retirement funds between organizations, organizational units, or individuals, or when large groups of Canadians lack the ability to support themselves after retirement, a distinct lack of parity could negatively affect every stakeholder. That's why this issue has been a cause for ongoing political and corporate debate since the 1980s.[2]

But the problem is that, despite this debate, very little has been done to change the status quo. Only in recent years have solutions to these challenges become more effective. In Canadian organizations, pension parity is now perceived as a pension obligation. In the future, that means that pension managers will need to develop their pension parity skills more than ever before.

In this chapter we'll look at what pension parity really means, and how organizations can protect themselves against the risk of parity issues, both financial and litigious. We'll talk about why parity, if it can be achieved, can drive both solutions and hope. Finally, we'll discuss why pension managers are the best equipped to take a key role in creating functional, operationalized changes in pensions that can impact equity in their organizations, the working world, and beyond.

What does pension parity really mean?

According to the Canadian Bar Association, pension parity doesn't exist, because there are vast differences between Registered Pension Plans (RPPs), namely, those received by employees of large organizations, and Registered Retirement Savings Plans (RRSPs), namely, savings opportunities offered by financial institutions.[3] There are also differences between the CPP and these other types of pensions. Finally, there are differences in access to pension types, and between who receives the benefits of pensions.

Let's unpack these ideas further.

In comparing RPPs and RRSPs, it's clear that the RPPs present a much lower risk to the individual. Because these are managed retirement plans and come with the kinds of economies of scale that can lower overall costs for each person involved in the plan, they are relatively safe investments. This is especially the case for defined benefit plans, but as a whole, defined contribution plans are still likely to result in a more risk-averse savings portfolio than RRSPs. RRSPs, often in the form of mutual funds, may result in a negative financial balance over the course of a contributor's lifetime, especially if the financial advice they are receiving is focused on investment growth over safety. RPPs present a more equitable option for retirees than RRSPs. Although many individuals who are self-employed or work for small businesses may never have the opportunity to join an RPP at all, this remains a best practice for retirement.

But this doesn't mean that RPPs always result in pension parity. Loopholes to parity have been found in some of the largest funds in the world, both corporate and public.

In 2019, it was found that, in the UK, the Teachers' Pension Scheme, an RPP, does not provide gender parity for the beneficiaries of its deceased members. Widows of male teachers over fifty years of age get more in survivor benefits than the widowers of female teachers with the same years of service, and similar disparities were found for same-sex spouses.[4] In other words, before this was noticed, females benefitted more than males when their spouse died, whether that spouse was male or female.

Although changes are being made, the reality is that many such invisible inequities in long-term plans remain hidden until members discover them.

In France, a different set of inequities began being debated in the public sector when it was found that a French woman receives an average gross monthly RPP payment of €1,123 compared with an average of €1,933 for a man.[5] Some of this inequity was discovered to be the result of occupational inequalities between men and women that persist over the course of their lifetimes, but the research also showed that women work for more years over the course of their careers than men, even accounting for childrearing time off, and work later in life, which means that they receive less money for more effort as a whole.[6]

Corporate risk-taking also decreases parity in fundamental ways. Corporations often try to have their cake and eat it too when it comes to addressing even the simplest parity issues, according to field research.[7] Most companies invest over 90 per cent of the risk portion of their portfolios to high-risk assets, which "has been damaging to wealth creation over the last decade and there are few signs for a reversal of fortune in the future."[8] This means that they are creating a situation where pension members feel as if they are safe in their future retirement, but they are not. Just like public service employees who think they are covered for retirement but in fact are affected by structural issues that prevent equity, corporate pension members, under these high-risk schemes, are affected by a deep and unknown insecurity.

What happens when issues like this arise? The risk is that the fund could be sued, collectively or individually. Very few pension schemes have fully hedged their liabilities when it comes to equity and parity, leaving most with a negative exposure to risk.

Parity and leadership

Parity is not only about doing what is right but also about securing ourselves against future risk. Pension managers need to be proactive about parity, because safer assets must offer higher risk-adjusted returns than riskier assets or, at the very least, proactively engage members in understanding just what it is they are investing in every paycheque.

Parity can be addressed by building bigger plans, and creating co-investment opportunities that drive up security. For example, in 2019 a number of new pension merger cases addressed some parity issues through shifts to joint risk/jointly sponsored plans. But even in these cases, do employees and employers truly understand what are sustainable solutions and filter out outdated myths about the value and parity of their pensions?

Most pension members do not spend a great deal of time thinking about or recognizing the lack of parity in their pensions until it is too late. Pension managers should never lose sight of this reality, because the repercussions for organizations could be very challenging. Addressing pension parity creates balance, because novel or unknown risk exposures are accounted for, and classes of risk can be better diversified and understood.

Managing risk is primarily a matter of leadership in pension management. Careful planning is not simply about the creation of financial security but also about the development of a values orientation that emphasizes meeting the realistic (rather than ideal) expectations of all pension contributors. Pension parity isn't simply about mitigating one set of risks, namely, those introduced by the market and companies in which we invest, but also about looking at the large-scale changes to the way we manage employees and do business, and how these shifts will continue to manifest in the future. It's about creating a cycle of risk management that is informed by employee engagement, training, mutual support, and personal and corporate development. The bottom line?

Those responsible for creating pensions ought to make sure that risks and differences between pension expectations and outcomes are minimized. Why? Because, as pension managers, we're becoming increasingly aware that what we do right now has repercussions a long way into the future, both socially and financially.

Operationalize parity now

The World Economic Forum suggests that organizations, both public and private, ought to take on several proactive solutions to underline parity in pension planning going forward.[9]

Recognize differences

There are differences in the way that people retire, depending on not only their age, gender, physical location, and social status but also how they plan for the future. A strategic approach to risk management requires pension managers to actively look for the ways that pension options, communications, and training target stereotypical employees versus all employees. How can leaders create opportunities to target vulnerable pension contributors so that they have a better chance of reaching pension parity, and so that the organization is not exposed to future risk?

Understand how the traditional workplace is changing

Many organizations now provide options for employees to take time off for extended family leave and sabbaticals.

Some multinational companies allow employees to move to different organizational locations that require different pension set-ups. Pension leadership needs either to allow people to continue to contribute while on leave, or to help pension members at the very least understand, and otherwise manage, the impact of lost years of contributions or tax limitations based on their life choices.

Develop a plan for disruption

As we've discussed in previous chapters, the future of work is significantly changing, and this will disproportionately affect workers in service roles, especially in the public sector, as noted by the World Economic Forum. Technology disruption, re-skilling, and shifting workplace norms need to be planned for, and leaders need to be aware of how this may affect pension contributions, especially over the next ten to twenty years, so that they can abate risk.

Raise awareness about financial security

Both pension members and pension managers must have a clear idea of what is required for retirement. Spouses cannot guarantee each other a retirement any longer, and financial and pension systems need to adjust as a whole. It is not enough to offer equity to all pension members and their partners. Organizations need to offer support to individuals to manage their financial independence after retirement.

Pension parity drives solutions and hope

The issue of pension parity runs deep. It's not simply about abating risk, but also about the broader strategy of how pension leaders think about the future of managing employees, contributions, and retirement.

As the Canadian Bar Association and the World Economic Forum suggest, there needs to be an end to the disparity between different pension options, if only because the world of finance and the future of work are changing so quickly that people aren't nearly as prepared for their retirement as they think they are. Those offering up pensions, from defined benefit plans to defined contribution plans to CPP, need to be aware that they bear the responsibility of critically examining *parity* in order to address *disparity* proactively. Corporate risk-taking and old-fashioned imbalances in opportunities have to be set aside in a world where transparency is becoming the norm.

Parity in pension management is both solution-oriented and hope-giving for pension members.

It's solution-oriented because taking a parity approach mitigates large-scale future risks for pensions and organizations, and because it presents clear criteria for digging into both the causes and effects of these risks. We need a more nuanced, clarity-oriented, and transparent approach to pension management, and leaning in to pension parity issues helps provide a better go-forward strategy for leaders in the field.

Pension parity is hope-giving because it also shifts the focus towards a future where people will have the means to retire with dignity and support. Emphasizing parity, therefore, also decreases the future financial onus on the public sector to provide for the elderly in society, and creates a stronger foundation for personal, occupational, and retirement wellness.

Pension managers taking a leadership position will act to develop their pension parity knowledge and skills. Starting now, we need to create the right foundation for pension development, erasing the mistakes of the past and moving in a direction that is smart, future-oriented, and balanced.

CONCLUSION: THE FUTURE DEPENDS ON US

WE ALL NEED a secure financial future. It seems to be a simple equation: provide people with a secure source of income and they'll be happier and more productive at work, knowing that most of their worries will be taken care of if they just stick with it.

But what happens if employees don't think about pensions in the way that we expect? What if the money they receive when they retire or leave the firm isn't the incentive or security blanket leaders believe it to be? And what if the people who manage our pension standards, our boards, aren't clued in to what really matters, both financially and in terms of the future of work?

Most business leaders don't usually step back and look at all the other factors that will affect pensions over time and that can put their business at risk in unexpected ways. A firm can follow a risk-based approach, therefore, and rely on actuaries to try to churn the numbers in the right way to make decisions, but this is only the first and most basic step forward. Actuarial tables only present us with a solution that is based on quantitative science.

As we've discussed earlier, just as an engineer building a bridge using only statistics needs to consider what happens in the case of an earthquake rather than just what happens during the average rush hour, leaders also need to consider the likelihood of a large-scale event obstructing perfect predictions in pension management. With medical science and big data, we may be able to better pinpoint individual lifespans and what the optimal age of retirement should be, but we still need to take this data with a grain of salt.

When it comes to predicting market performance and viability over the long term, conventional methods tend to fail more often than not, which is why a leadership orientation to pension management is key. Leaders can choose broader and more unconventional methods to get to the heart of the data and to use it in the right way to build a pension plan that will last, and limit their exposure. A leader can bring the conversation back to risk, market performance, and viability over time to shift the focus of the work towards what their business needs rather than what an actuary thinks is important. Pension leadership decisions also need to incorporate new definitions of fiduciary duty and public trust that consider both local and global ideals as the law shifts to accommodate new definitions of legal business responsibilities around the world.

Pensions are, ultimately, a long-term game.

How can you pay attention to the right details? How can you make sure that everyone, including those inside and outside the management team, has the tools needed to connect and engage? Is it even possible to create a culture aligned with pension planning excellence? It is possible to nudge both private and public sector organizations towards a new way of thinking about retirement, pensions, and the game of understanding what matters to our futures, and the future of work. But as this book has demonstrated, only broader, leadership-oriented approaches, rather than pension-only approaches, can help alleviate standard barriers and build forward effectively.

Adaptation to the future of work is likely a necessary shift for most organizations. They will need to be able to position themselves strategically in newly competitive labour markets, because, more and more, demand for skilled employees is on the rise. Workers are becoming choosier, especially when they know that a range of work options are available to them. Organizations are going to have to become significantly more agile in the way they think about managing people's work and about the workforce as a whole as they move towards the future. The hunt for talent, and tapping into the right pension strategy, can be as simple as talking to that talent. Collaboration is a key part of getting the data that organizations need to make decisions that will work for them. But the challenge is more complex than that: organizations need to look at the big picture. To develop healthy, well-performing pensions that work for future employees, it is necessary to look at pension planning from several different angles—in terms of psychological safety, portability, ethical standards, and parity. Future employees will want the ability to collaborate with their organizational leaders to develop a pension plan that matches their future goals. Employees may want more flexibility, more portability, and more fund transparency than they have aimed for in the past.

For organizations, this means thinking differently about pensions: pensions operate not only as funding for retirement, but also as a means to gain employee trust and engagement. Technological solutions for pension planning may be able to provide us with deeper data, better engagement, and more successful plans for companies and pension investors alike. Technology can help us create retirement plans for young people so that they can protect their future. It can help companies drive down costs of pension management and tailor plans to the individual.

Underneath the surface, however, pension managers have the responsibility to build equity into our plans by turning a critical eye to what matters now, and what will matter in the future, to pension members. It's about creating a cycle of risk management informed by employee engagement, training, mutual support, and personal and corporate development.

When we make decisions for our pensions, we have a large-scale impact on our society. That means that pension management isn't just about one business and one set of employees, but also about how we manage the steps we take towards the future.

In an ever-evolving world, we can make a difference through strategic pension management. But actualizing the future that we want to see depends wholly on our ability to lead.

NOTES

Introduction

1 B. Kochkodin and L. Meisler, "S&P 500's Biggest Pension Plans Face $382 Billion Funding Gap," Bloomberg, July 20, 2017, https://www.bloomberg.com/graphics/2017-corporate-pensions/.

Chapter 1

1 Sophia Harris, "Sears Pensioners Hope to Recoup Their Losses in $509M Lawsuit," CBC News, December 4, 2018, https://www.cbc.ca/news/business/sears-canada-retirees-pension-eddie-lampert-court-1.4930785.
2 Roger Lowenstein, *While America Aged: How Pension Debt Ruined General Motors, Stopped the NYC Subways, Bankrupted San Diego, and Looms as the Next Financial Crisis* (New York: Penguin Group, 2008).
3 Matt Egan, "GE's $31 Billion Pension Nightmare," CNN, January 19, 2018, https://money.cnn.com/2018/01/18/investing/ge-pension-immelt-breakup/index.html.
4 Jamie Golombek quoted in Karina Roman, "Your Tax Bill Could Change in 2019. Here's What to Expect," CBC News, December

31, 2018, https://www.cbc.ca/news/politics/tax-changes-cra-canada-1.4944505.

5 Kenneth David Strang and Narasimha Rao Vajjhala, "Impact of Socialized Uncertainty on Group Decision Making: An Experiment with Emerging Executives," *International Journal of Risk and Contingency Management (IJRCM)* 4, no. 2 (2015): 45–58.

6 Olivia S. Mitchell, P. Brett Hammond, and Stephen P. Utkus, eds., *Financial Decision Making and Retirement Security in an Aging World* (Oxford: Oxford University Press, 2017).

7 Mitchell, Hammond, and Utkus, eds., "Financial Decision Making."

8 Marc Lee and Justin Ritchie, *Pension Funds and Fossil Fuels: The Economic Case for Divestment* (Ottawa: Canadian Centre for Policy Alternatives, 2015), https://www.policyalternatives.ca/publications/reports/pension-funds-and-fossil-fuels.

9 "Global Economics Update," Capital Economics, accessed December 2018, capitaleconomics.com; Lee and Ritchie, *Pension Funds.*

Chapter 2

1 Jim C. Collins, *How the Mighty Fall: And Why Some Companies Never Give In* (New York: Random House, 2009).

2 James Gregory and Hampton Bridwell, "Innovative Disruption: Utilising Brand to Manage and Drive Change," *Journal of Brand Strategy* 5, no. 2 (2016): 142–49.

3 Gregory and Bridwell, 142–49.

4 B. Rajesh Kumar, Dhruv Arora, and Akshay Bansal, "Valuation of General Electric: A Case Analysis," *International Journal of Teaching and Case Studies* 6, no. 3 (2015): 183–98.

5 Sean Stein Smith, "The Financial Effects of Strategic Divestment—An Analysis of GE Capital," *Accounting and Finance Research* 6, no. 4 (2017): 244.

6 Matt Egan, "Everything Is Shrinking at GE Except Its Massive Debt," CNN Money, March 16, 2018, https://money.cnn.com/2018/03/16/investing/ge-stock-debt/index.html.

7 Egan, "Everything Is Shrinking."

8 Alwyn Scott and Ankit Ajmera, "GE Offers to Buy Back at Least $9 Billion in Debt, Plans New Longer-Maturities Issue," Reuters, April 13, 2020, https://fr.reuters.com/article/us-health-coronavirus-ge-idUSKCN21V1AW.
9 "Steel Baron Andrew Carnegie Pioneered Pension Funding," *Pensions & Investment*, December 27, 1999, 34, https://www.pionline.com/article/19991227/PRINT/912270706/steel-baron-andrew-carnegie-pioneered-pension-funding.

Chapter 3

1 Andrew Russell, "Is Canada's Health-Care System Ready for Our Rapidly Greying Population?" Global News, May 5, 2017, https://globalnews.ca/news/3429041/healthcare-stats-canada-2016-census/.
2 "Canada Population Live," Worldometer, accessed August 18, 2020, https://www.worldometers.info/world-population/canada-population/.
3 Pattie Lovett-Reid, "32% of Canadians Are Nearing Retirement without Any Savings: Poll," BNN Bloomberg, February 8, 2019, https://www.bnnbloomberg.ca/32-of-canadians-are-nearing-retirement-without-any-savings-poll-1.991680.
4 Jason Powell and Jon Hendricks, "The Sociological Construction of Ageing: Lessons for Theorising," *International Journal of Sociology and Social Policy* 29 (2009): 84–94.
5 Judith Graham, "How to Beat the Stereotypes around Aging," CNN, November 14, 2017, http://www.cnn.com/2017/11/14/health/beat-aging-stereotypes-partner/index.html.
6 Roy Romanow, *Building on Values, the Future of Healthcare in Canada* (Ottawa: Government of Canada, 2002).
7 "Ministry Plans," Ontario Ministry of Health and Long Term Care, last modified October 6, 2016, http://www.health.gov.on.ca/en/common/ministry/publications/plans/ppar16/.
8 "Selected Characteristics of Tax Filters with Registered Retirement Savings Plan (RRSP) Contributions," Statistics Canada, last modified August 24, 2020, https://www150.statcan.gc.ca/t1/tbl1/en/tv.action?pid=1110004401.

9 René Morissette and Anick Johnson, "Are Good Jobs Disappearing in Canada?" Statistics Canada, Business and Labour Market Analysis Division, January 26, 2005, https://www150.statcan.gc.ca/n1/en/catalogue/11F0019M2005239.
10 Lucian Bebchuk and Jesse Fried, *Pay without Performance: The Unfulfilled Promise of Executive Compensation* (Cambridge, MA: Harvard University Press, 2004).
11 Olivia Mitchell and Stephen Utkus, "Lessons from Behavioral Finance for Retirement Plan Design" (Pension Research Council Working Paper 2003-6, University of Pennsylvania, Philadelphia, 2003).
12 Dennis Raphael, *Poverty in Canada: Implications for Health and Quality of Life*, 2nd ed. (Toronto: Canadian Scholars' Press, 2011).

Chapter 4

1 Kathleen Vohs, Nicole Mead, and Miranda Goode, "The Psychological Consequences of Money," *Science* 314 (2006): 1154–56.
2 Carol Nickerson, Norbert Schwarz, Ed Diener, and Daniel Kahneman, "Zeroing In on the Dark Side of the American Dream: A Closer Look at the Negative Consequences of the Goal for Financial Success," *Psychological Science* 14, no. 6 (2003): 531–36.
3 Elizabeth Dunn, Lara B. Aknin, and Michael I. Norton, "Spending Money on Others Promotes Happiness," *Science* 319 (2008): 1687–88.
4 Day Manoli and Andrea Weber, "Nonparametric Evidence on the Effects of Financial Incentives on Retirement Decisions," *American Economic Journal: Economic Policy* 8, no. 4 (2016): 160–82. Although there are other, more frequent benefits such as extended and basic health care plans, these are not considered to be financial benefits.
5 Abraham Maslow, "A Theory of Human Motivation," *Psychological Review* 50, no. 4 (1943): 370–96.
6 A. Wigfield and J. Eccles, "The Development of Achievement Task Values: A Theoretical Analysis," *Developmental Review* 12 (1992): 265–310.
7 Melissa A. Knoll, "Behavioral and Psychological Aspects of the Retirement Decision," *Social Security Bulletin* 71, no. 4 (2011): 15.

8 Douglas A. Hershey, Joy M. Jacobs-Lawson, John J. McArdle, and Fumiaki Hamagami, "Psychological Foundations of Financial Planning for Retirement," *Journal of Adult Development* 14, no. 1–2 (2007): 26–36.
9 Xijing Wang and Eva G. Krumhuber, "The Love of Money Results in Objectification," *British Journal of Social Psychology* 56, no. 2 (2017): 354–72.
10 Vohs, Mead, and Goode, "Psychological Consequences," 1154–56.
11 Elisaveta Gjorgji Sardžoska and Thomas Li-Ping Tang, "Monetary Intelligence: Money Attitudes—Unethical Intentions, Intrinsic and Extrinsic Job Satisfaction, and Coping Strategies across Public and Private Sectors in Macedonia," *Journal of Business Ethics* 130, no. 1 (2015): 93–115.
12 Ahmed Elsayed, Andries de Grip, Didier Fouarge, and Raymond Montizaan, "Gradual Retirement, Financial Incentives, and Labour Supply of Older Workers: Evidence from a Stated Preference Analysis," *Journal of Economic Behavior & Organization* 150 (2018): 277–94.

Chapter 5

1 Nicole Gibillini, "Canada's Actuaries Urge Governments to Raise Retirement Age," BNN Bloomberg, April 15, 2019, https://www.bnnbloomberg.ca/canada-s-actuaries-urge-governments-to-raise-retirement-age-1.1244550.
2 João Filipe Clérigo Ribeiro de Almeida, "Genetic Algorithms Applied to Asset and Liability Management" (master's thesis, Nova Information Management School, 2016), https://pdfs.semanticscholar.org/2701/6c411691f21ed4010426bda66aa9d088c0d2.pdf.
3 Nabil Abu El Ata and Rudolf Schmandt, *The Tyranny of Uncertainty: A New Framework to Predict, Remediate and Monitor Risk* (London: Springer, 2016).
4 Edouard Debonneuil, Stéphanie Loisel, and Frédéric Planchet, "Do Actuaries Believe in Longevity Deceleration?" *Insurance: Mathematics and Economics* 78 (2018): 325–38.
5 De Almeida, "Genetic Algorithms," 1.

6 "CAAT Plan Wins Pension Performance Award for Membership Growth Strategy," CAAT Pension Plan, October 25, 2018, https://www.caatpension.ca/members/member-news/member-news-listing/CAAT-Plan-wins-pension-performance-award-for-membership-growth-strategy.
7 Alexey Turchin and David Denkenberger, "Global Catastrophic and Existential Risks Communication Scale," *Futures* 102 (2018): 27–38.

Chapter 6

1 Elizabeth Shilton, *Empty Promises: Why Workplace Pension Law Doesn't Deliver Pensions* (Montreal, Kingston: McGill-Queen's University Press, 2016).
2 E. Philip Davis and Rosa M. Lastra, *Pension Provision, Care and Dignity in Old Age: Legal and Economic Issues* (London: Brunel University London, 2016), https://papers.ssrn.com/sol3/papers.cfm?abstract_id=2780484.
3 Marta Ballester, Dov Fried, and Joshua Livnat, *Pension Plan Contributions, Free Cash Flows and Financial Slack* (unpublished working paper, New York University, 2002), Word document.
4 Elizabeth Shilton, "Employee Pension Rights and the False Promise of Trust Law," *Dalhousie Law Journal* 34 (2011): 81.
5 John Braithwaite, *Restorative Justice and Responsive Regulation* (New York: Oxford University Press, 2002).
6 Archibald MacLeish, "Apologia," *Harvard Law Review* 85, no. 8 (1972): 1505–11.
7 David Zhou, "Re Indalex: The Confluence of Pension, Insolvency, and Fiduciary Law," *Dalhousie Journal of Legal Studies* 25 (2016): 137.
8 Davis and Lastra, "Pension Provision," 8.
9 Eva Maria Hohnerlein, "Pension Indexation for Retirees Revisited—Normative Patterns and Legal Standards," *Global Social Policy* 19, no. 3 (2019): 246–65.
10 Zhou, "Re Indalex," 149.
11 Markus Höllerer, *Between Creed, Rhetoric Façade, and Disregard: Dissemination and Theorization of Corporate Social Responsibility in Austria* (Frankfurt: Peter Lang GmbH, Internationaler Verlag der Wissenschaften, 2012).

12 Maria Teresa Bosch-Badia, Joan Montllor-Serrats, and Maria Antonia Tarrazon, "Corporate Social Responsibility from Friedman to Porter and Kramer," *Theoretical Economics Letters* 3 no. 3A (2013): 11.
13 Bosch-Badia, Montllor-Serrats, and Tarrazon, 11.
14 Höllerer, *Between Creed*, 31.
15 Cynthia A. Williams, "Corporate Social Responsibility and Corporate Governance," in Oxford *Handbook of Corporate Law and Governance*, ed. Jeffrey N. Gordon and Wolf-Georg Ringe (Oxford: Oxford University Press, 2018), 634–77. Chapter available at https://ssrn.com/abstract=2635473.
16 Cynthia A. Williams and John M. Conley, "Is There an Emerging Fiduciary Duty to Consider Human Rights?" *University of Cincinnati Law Review* 74, no. 1 (2005): 76.

Chapter 7

1 Kelsey Rolfe, "Border Officers' Union Calls for 25-and-Out Pension," Benefits Canada, June 19, 2019, https://www.benefitscanada.com/news/border-guards-union-calls-for-25-and-out-pension-131860.
2 Rolfe, "Border Officers."
3 Ali Noruzy, Vahid Majazi Dalfard, Benhaz Azhdari, Salman Nazari-Shirkouhi, and Aliasghar Rezazadeh, "Relations between Transformational Leadership, Organizational Learning, Knowledge Management, Organizational Innovation, and Organizational Performance: An Empirical Investigation of Manufacturing Firms," *The International Journal of Advanced Manufacturing Technology* (2013): 1–13.
4 Peter G. Northouse, *Leadership: Theory and Practice*, 6th ed. (Thousand Oaks, CA: Sage Publications, 2013).
5 Yueng-Hsiang Huang, Jin Lee, Anna C. McFadden, Lauren A. Murphy, Michelle M. Robertson, Janelle H. Cheung, and Dov Zohar, "Beyond Safety Outcomes: An Investigation of the Impact of Safety Climate on Job Satisfaction, Employee Engagement and Turnover Using Social Exchange Theory as the Theoretical Framework," *Applied Ergonomics* 55 (2016): 248–57.
6 Juan A. Moriano, Fernando Molero, Gabriela Topa, and Jean-Pierre Lévy Mangin, "The Influence of Transformational Leadership and

Organizational Identification on Intrapreneurship," *International Entrepreneurship and Management Journal* 10, no. 1 (2014): 118.
7 C. Boykins, S. Campbell, M. Moore, and S. Nayyar, "An Empirical Study of Leadership Styles," *Journal of Economic Development, Management, IT, Finance & Marketing* 5, no. 2 (2013): 1–10.
8 Jennifer Paterson, "How Air Canada's Pension Took Off as Canada Post's Plan Sank into Deficit," Benefits Canada, April 15, 2016, https://www.benefitscanada.com/news/how-air-canadas-pension-took-off-as-canada-posts-plan-sank-into-deficit-79555.
9 Paterson, "How Air Canada's Pension Took Off."
10 Oli R. Mihalache, Justin J. Jansen, Frans A. Van den Bosch, and H.W. Volberda, "Top Management Team Shared Leadership and Organizational Ambidexterity: A Moderated Mediation Framework," *Strategic Entrepreneurship Journal* 8, no. 2 (2014): 128–48.
11 Christopher B. Dobni and Mark Klassen, "Advancing an Innovation Orientation in Organizations: Insights from North American Business Leaders," *Journal of Innovation Management* 3, no. 1 (2015): 104–21.

Chapter 8

1 "Multi-Country Survey Finds Most Workers Cite Pension and Retirement Benefits as Critical Factor When Deciding to Accept or Stay in a Job," BusinessWire, July 11, 2019, https://www.businesswire.com/news/home/20190711005002/en/Multi-Country-Survey-Finds-Workers-Cite-Pension-Retirement.
2 *The Future of Jobs: Employment, Skills and Workforce Strategy for the Fourth Industrial Revolution* (Geneva: World Economic Forum, 2016), http://www3.weforum.org/docs/WEF_Future_of_Jobs.pdf.
3 Jill Rubery, Damian Grimshaw, Arjan Keizer, and Matthew Johnson, "Challenges and Contradictions in the 'Normalising' of Precarious Work," *Work, Employment and Society* 32, no. 3 (2018): 509–27.
4 Mathias Czaika and Hein de Haas, "The Globalisation of Migration: Has the World Become More Migratory?" *International Migration Review* 48, no. 2 (2014): 283–323.

5 Rebecca Campbell, "The Cost of Choice: Should We Be Free to Choose When It Comes to Our Pension?" (PhD diss., London School of Economics and Political Science, 2018).
6 Edward Lawler, "Organizations Should Put Talent First," *Huffington Post*, January 22, 2017, http://www.huffingtonpost.com/ed-lawler/organizations-should-put_b_14323730.html.
7 Jack Kelly, "Top CEOs Sign a Statement Prioritizing People over Profits: What It Means for Employees," *Forbes*, August 20, 2019, https://www.forbes.com/sites/jackkelly/2019/08/20/top-ceos-sign-a-radical-statement-prioritizing-employees-over-profits/#44555385581b.
8 Slavina Spasova and Bart Vanhercke, *The 'Generosity' of Pensions for Workers in Hard Jobs: In Need of a Nuanced Debate* (Brussels: ETUI Research Paper-Policy Brief, 2018), https://www.etui.org/sites/default/files/Pensions%20hard%20jobs%20Spasova%20Vanhercke%20Policy%20Brief%202018.12.pdf.
9 Adam M. Grant, "Leading with Meaning: Beneficiary Contact, Prosocial Impact, and the Performance Effects of Transformational Leadership," *Academy of Management Journal* 55, no. 2 (2012): 458–76.
10 George Milkovich, Jerry Newman, and Barry Gerhart, *Compensation*, 11th ed. (New York: McGraw-Hill Irwin, 2014).
11 *Future of Jobs*, 29.
12 Scott Sweatman, *20 Questions Directors Should Ask about Pension Governance* (Toronto: Canadian Institute of Chartered Accountants, 2017).

Chapter 9

1 Jeremy Peat, Owen Kelly, and Daniel Broby, *Fintech: Hype or Reality?* (Glasgow: International Public Policy Institute [IPPI], University of Strathclyde, 2017).
2 "IOPS International Conference on Pension Supervision and Regulation 2019," IOPS, March 7, 2019, http://www.iopsweb.org/iops-international-conference-pension-supervision-regulation-2019.htm.
3 *The Global Findex Database* (Washington, DC: World Bank, 2017).

4 Kelvin Leong and Anna Sung, "FinTech (Financial Technology): What Is It and How to Use Technologies to Create Business Value in Fintech Way?" *International Journal of Innovation, Management and Technology* 9, no. 2 (2018): 74–78.
5 Barbara Alemanni, "From Nudging to Engaging in Pension," in *Challenges in Ensuring Financial Competencies*, ed. Nadia Linciano and Paolo Soccorso (Rome: Consob, 2017), http://www.consob.it/documents/46180/46181/wp84.pdf/c369a6db-3b30-4c1a-8a90-d3f2d384ec4f. From the International Organization of Securities Commissions (IOSCO) conference, October 2–8, 2017, Rome, Italy.
6 "How to Do Business More Securely and in Compliance," Microsoft, accessed August 20, 2020, https://www.microsoft.com/en-ca/industry/financial-services/banking-and-capital-markets.
7 Leong and Sung, "FinTech," 74–78.
8 Matt Egan, "GE's $31 Billion Pension Nightmare," CNN, January 19, 2018, https://money.cnn.com/2018/01/18/investing/ge-pension-immelt-breakup/index.html.
9 Alex Mazer, *The Future of Pensions in Uncertain Times: 2018 CPPLC Pension Forum Rapporteur's Report* (Ottawa: Canadian Public Pension Leadership Council, 2018), http://cpplc.ca/wp-content/uploads/2019/02/the-future-of-pensions-in-uncertain-times.pdf.

Chapter 10

1 George Apostolakis, Frido Kraanen, and Gert van Dijk, "Pension Beneficiaries' and Fund Managers' Perceptions of Responsible Investment: A Focus Group Study," *Corporate Governance: The International Journal of Business in Society* 16, no. 1 (2016): 1–20.
2 Leonardo Weiss-Cohen, Peter Ayton, Iain Clacher, and Volker Thoma, "Behavioral Biases in Pension Fund Trustees' Decision Making," *Review of Behavioral Finance* 11, no. 1 (2019).
3 Susan Sayce, Johanna Weststar, and Anil Verma, "The Recruitment and Selection of Pension Trustees: An Integrative Approach," *Human Resource Management Journal* 24, no. 3 (2014): 307–22.

4 Weiss-Cohen, Ayton, Clacher, and Thoma, "Behavioral Biases."
5 N. Chambers, G. Harvey, R. Mannion, J. Bond, and J. Marshall, "Theories About Boards," *Health Services and Delivery Research* 1, no. 6 (2013): 1–19.
6 Helena Isidro and Márcia Sobral, "The Effects of Women on Corporate Boards on Firm Value, Financial Performance, and Ethical and Social Compliance," *Journal of Business Ethics* 132, no. 1 (2015): 1–19.
7 John Greenwood, "Well-Run Firms Have Women on Board: Downe," *Financial Post,* October 17, 2011, https://financialpost.com/news/fp-street/well-run-firms-have-women-on-board-downe.
8 Sayce, Weststar, and Verma, "Recruitment and Selection," 307–22.
9 Sharon Hendricks, Jay C. Rehak, and Dan Pedrotty, "The 7 Attributes of Highly Effective Pension Trustees," Trustee Leadership Forum for Retirement Security, accessed August 24, 2020, https://iri.hks.harvard.edu/files/iri/files/seven-attributes-one-page-summary.pdf.
10 Keith L. Johnson and Frank Jan de Graaf, "Modernizing Pension Fund Legal Standards for the Twenty-First Century," *Rotman International Journal of Pension Management* 2, no. 1 (2009).
11 Chambers, Harvey, Mannion, Bond, and Marshall, "Theories about Boards," 1–19.

Chapter 11

1 Edward Qian, *Risk Parity Fundamentals* (Boca Raton, FL: CRC Press, 2018).
2 Canadian Bar Association, *The Need for Pension Parity* (Ottawa: Canadian Bar Association, 2001).
3 *The Need for Pension Parity* (Ottawa: RRSP Alliance, 2001), https://www.cba.org/CMSPages/GetFile.aspx?guid=58df371f-5594-4ce8-a866-f2c83544608e.
4 "Survivor's Benefits in the Teachers' Pension Scheme," Teachers' Pensions, last updated March 29, 2018, https://www.teacherspensions.co.uk/news/public-news/2018/03/survivors-benefits-in-the-teachers-pension-scheme.aspx.

5 Aude Mazoue, "French Women May Be the Biggest Losers under Macron's Pension Reform Plan," France 24, October 12, 2019, https://www.france24.com/en/20191210-french-women-may-be-the-big-losers-under-macron-s-pension-reform-plan-france-1.

6 Stephanie Lane, "The Scary Facts behind the Gender Pension Gap," World Economic Forum, March 7, 2018, https://www.weforum.org/agenda/2018/03/retired-women-less-money-pensions-than-men/.

7 Edward Qian, "Risk Parity and Diversification," *Journal of Investing* 20, no. 1, 119–27.

8 Qian, "Risk Parity and Diversification," 126.

9 *The Future of Jobs: Employment, Skills and Workforce Strategy for the Fourth Industrial Revolution* (Geneva: World Economic Forum, 2016), http://www3.weforum.org/docs/WEF_Future_of_Jobs.pdf.

ACKNOWLEDGEMENTS

THANK YOU TO my past and current clients. I've worked with managers and executives who truly take the time to make good decisions for their pension plans and their people.

Also thank you to my colleagues in the pension industry. I've been fortunate to have worked with excellent companies as clients, pension lawyers, and actuaries who share our client value and passion for pension services. They have inspired my work and this book.

INDEX

ABOUT THE AUTHOR

M. CATHERINE MILLER, FSA, ACIA, the managing partner of Marris + Miller, brings transformational, democratic leadership to pension planning and strategy. Knowing that our pension systems constitute the world's largest reserve of capital, Catherine realizes that pensions are more than a group of individual retirement plans. Not only does strategic pension management provide pension planners and future retirees with a sense of security in their futures, but Catherine suggests that we also need to recognize pensions' role in the overarching way our businesses, and our global economy, are run. Pensions need to provide hope for the future, and business leaders need to create capacity for change so that a balance between risk and outcomes serves all stakeholders. Actuarial science may be complex, but Marris + Miller provides strategic options that work. Through the firm's visionary work in this field, Catherine provides clarity on some of the most complex issues of the day: while pension plans in some of the world's largest companies are failing, Marris + Miller looks at how to build transparency and accountability into every level of pension management, so that businesses and the people who run them and work for them can remain confident in their choices. Catherine believes that leadership is the pathway to a new way of looking at pensions, where strategic thinking and transformational visioning result in healthy companies, ready to take on a new generation of positive and sustainable business change.

Made in United States
Orlando, FL
04 November 2026

90205154R00141